ARDEN'S HOU

4

Series Editors: Andrew Arden QC and Caroline Hunter

Andrew Dymond is a practising barrister at Arden Chambers, specialising in housing, landlord and tenant, and local government law. He contributes articles on housing law to various legal journals and is the author of *Security of Tenure: law and practice in the management of social housing* (Arden's Housing Library, vol 1).

PRESENTING POSSESSION PROCEEDINGS

LAW AND PRACTICE IN THE MANAGEMENT OF SOCIAL HOUSING

Andrew Dymond
BARRISTER

First published in Great Britain 1996 by

Lemos & Crane
20 Pond Square, Highgate
London N6 6BA

Telephone 0181 348 8263

ISBN 1-898001-15-4

A CIP catalogue record for this book is
available from the British Library.

Designed by Mick Keates.
Typeset by Concise Artisans, London.
Printed by Redwood Books, Trowbridge.

ARDEN'S HOUSING LIBRARY

Series Editors: Andrew Arden, QC and Caroline Hunter

"... an increasingly important series."
Housing (the journal of the Chartered Institute of Housing)

Other volumes already published in Arden's Housing Library

Vol. 1 *Security of Tenure* by Andrew Diamond
Vol. 2 *Tenants' Rights* by Caroline Hunter
Vol. 3 *Nuisance and Harassment* by Susan Belgrave

To place orders and for information about forthcoming volumes, please contact

Lemos & Crane
20 Pond Square
Highgate
London N6 6BA

Tel: 0181 348 8263
Fax: 0181 347 5740

CONTENTS

Table of Cases xi
Table of Statutes xii

INTRODUCTION 1

Part I. Possession Procedure: Commencement to Trial *5*

1 COMMENCING POSSESSION PROCEEDINGS 7
Steps before action 7
Termination of the tenancy agreement 8
Notice seeking possession 10
Choice of court 13
Summons and pleadings 14
The parties 20

2 WHAT NEEDS TO BE PROVED? 21
Ownership of the land 22
Proving the tenancy agreement 22
Termination of tenants' interest 23
Form of the notice 23
Service of the notice 23
Reason for seeking possession 26
Non-secure/assured tenants 26
Secure/assured tenants 26
Reasonableness 26
Suitable alternative accommodation 28
Money judgments 31
Checklists 32
Loss of security of tenure 32
Death of tenant 33
Notice to quit by joint tenant 33
Exceptions to security of tenure 34
Claims based on statutory grounds for possession 37

3 THE RETURN DATE 44
Nature of the hearing 44
Defences raised at return date 45
Typical outcomes at return date 46
Proving the case 47

Adjournments 48
Consolidation 51

4 PRETRIAL PROCEDURE 53
Directions: generally 54
Procedural steps 55
Pleadings 55
Discovery 58
Witness statements 60
Unless orders 62
Typical directions 63

5 EVIDENCE 65
Burden of proof 65
Types of evidence 66
Hearsay 67
Informal admission 69
Public documents 69
Evidence under Civil Evidence Act 70
Affidavit evidence 71
Expert evidence 72

6. THE TRIAL 75
Settlement 76
Judges 76
Giving evidence 77
The oath 77
The opening 77
Landlord's case 78
Evidence-in-chief 78
Cross-examination 78
Re-examination 80
Defence case 80
Closing speeches 81

Part II. Possession Procedure: Types of cases 83

7 RENT ARREARS CASES 85
Statutory grounds 85
Required evidence 87
Evidence of arrears 88

Options for orders 88
Arrears cleared 89
Arrears substantially cleared and agreement about remainder 89
Arrears at significant level 90
Very significant arrears 91
Defences 92
Disrepair 92
Housing benefit 93
Landlord and Tenant Act 1987 95

8 OTHER TYPES OF POSSESSION ACTION 96
Unauthorised occupiers 96
Required evidence 97
Defences 98
Money judgment 103
Return date 105
Nuisance and annoyance 106
Witness statement 110
Return date 110
Undertakings 110

9 LIMITED SECURITY 113
Assured shortholds 113
Accelerated possession procedure 114
Licensees 114
Summary possession 115

Part III. Possession Procedure: Orders and further action 121

10 POSSESSION ORDERS 123
Immediate order 123
Outright order 124
Suspended possession order 125
Order not to be enforced without leave 126
Money judgment 126
Consent order 126
Costs 129
Types of order 130
Costs orders at return date 132
Legal aid 133

11 FURTHER ACTION 134
Warrants for possession 134
Appeals 136
Stay of execution 137
Setting aside an order for possession 137
Subsequent conduct by parties 138

Part IV. Appendix: Court forms and glossary 141

Form N5 Summons for possession 143
Form N119 Particulars of claim (rent arrears) 144
Form N117 Undertaking 148
Form N26 Order for possession (assured tenancies) 150
Form N26 Order for possession (possession suspended/rented property) 152
Glossary of terms 154

CUMULATIVE INDEX 159

TABLE OF CASES

Bruce v Worthing Borough Council (1993)
26 HLR 223, CA *128, 129*
Burrows v Brent LBC (1995) 27 HLR 748, CA *140*

Dallhold Estates (UK) Pty. Inc. v Lindsey Trading Properties Inc.
[1994] 1 EGLR 93 CA *95*

Lambeth LBC v White 1995 June *Legal Action*, p19 *49, 67*
London Borough of Wandsworth v Fadayomi (1987)
19 HLR 512, CA *128*

Mountain v Hastings (1993) 25 HLR 427, CA *93*

Ottway v Jones [1955] 2 All ER 585 CA *130*

Rogan v Woodfield Building Services (1994)
27 HLR 78, CA *95*

Woking Borough Council v Bistram (1993) 27 HLR 1, CA *28*

TABLE OF STATUTES

Children Act 1989 *109*

Civil Evidence Act 1968
61, 70-71

County Courts Act 1984
s 21(1) *13*

Housing Act 1980
s 89 *124*
s 89(2)(c) *124*

Housing Act 1985 *9, 13, 23, 26, 28, 37, 106, 125, 127*
s 81 *32*
s 82(2) *139*
s 83(1) *24*
s 85(1) *90*
s 85(2) *137*
s 93(1) *99*
Sch 1 *9, 19, 34, 36*
Sch 1 para 2 *34*
Sch 1 para 3 *35*
Sch 2 *9, 10, 11, 18-19, 29, 39, 40, 41, 42, 66, 73, 85, 88, 127*

Housing Act 1988 *9, 13, 23, 26, 29, 30, 38, 106, 125, 127, 154*
s 1 *32*
s 8 *24*
s 8(1)(b) *24*
s 9(1) *90*
s 9(2) *137*
Sch 1 *9, 34*
Sch 2 *9, 19, 24, 29, 39, 42, 85*
Sch 2 Part III *30*

Landlord and Tenant Act 1987
s 48 *87, 95*
s 48(2) *95*

Law of Property Act 1925
s 146 *25*

Local Government and Housing Act 1989 *92*

Matrimonial Homes Act 1983
s 1(5) *98*

Social Security Contributions and Benefits Act 1992 *18*

Stamp Act 1891
s 14 *37*

INTRODUCTION

The aim of this book is to provide housing managers and officers with a guide to how possession proceedings are conducted, and to assist them in performing their role in obtaining the necessary evidence in various types of possession proceedings which are commonly encountered.

Whilst housing managers or officers does not require detailed knowledge of the intricacies of court procedure, they must know how court proceedings are conducted in order to be aware of (a) the evidence which is required to prove a case, and (b) the types of evidence which cannot be brought before a court. Greater knowledge of the basics of court procedure means that housing managers are more aware of the time scales involved, and the significance of particular applications which may be made, so that, when solicitors or an internal legal department request information, there is a better understanding of the purpose of the particular step in the preparation of the case as a whole.

Furthermore, it is now increasingly common for housing managers or officers to conduct simple possession actions themselves, in particular claims for possession based on rent arrears. It is vital that housing staff who do so are aware of the range of orders which may be made at the return date, in particular, when an adjournment can be granted, and the implications of the different orders as to costs. The book is intended to help those who may be asked to undertake such work.

In more complex possession actions housing managers or officers may be called as witnesses and again an understanding of what evidence is required to prove the case, and the issues which are important to the court, may assist managers in presenting the best evidence.

As the book is primarily concerned with questions of procedure and the gathering of evidence, the book does not purport to deal in detail with the substantive law of security tenure, and the rights of particular occupiers, although, inevitably, questions of security of tenure are touched upon. For further guidance as to the substantive law in this regard reference may be made to A. Dymond *Security of Tenure* Arden's Housing Library vol.1, 1995.

The book is divided into four parts. Part I concerns the procedure which should be followed from the commencement of proceedings through to trial, highlighting the evidence which housing managers need to consider, and obtain, and the court procedures involved. Part II addresses particular types of case commonly encountered by housing officers. Part III looks at the types of order which may be made by the courts, and any further applications by defendants which housing officers may have to address. Part IV is an appendix containing specimen forms and glossary of legal terms used in this guide.

County Court Rules

Throughout the book reference is made to various orders of the County Court Rules (CCR). These are the Rules of Court, which govern the procedures and powers of the county court.

PART I

POSSESSION PROCEDURE: COMMENCEMENT TO TRIAL

CHAPTER 1

COMMENCING POSSESSION PROCEEDINGS

Steps before action / Termination of the tenancy agreement / ***Notice seeking possession*** **/ Choice of court / Summons and pleadings /** ***Content of summons and particulars of claim*** **/ The parties**

This chapter concerns the considerations behind the decision to issue proceedings, the steps which need to be taken before proceedings are issued, and how to commence possession proceedings.

Steps before action

Possession proceedings should be viewed as a last resort. Every effort should be made to ensure that differences are resolved on a consensual basis before embarking upon the considerable costs involved in litigation. In certain cases, alternative forms of resolving disputes should be considered, eg mediation procedures for neighbour disputes. This approach is not only important for the avoidance of the costly process of court procedure, but also essential to the success of any case which does come to trial.

In the majority of cases which are brought by a social landlord against a tenant – whether secure or assured – the landlord must satisfy the court that it is reasonable for an order for possession to be made. Accordingly, it is vitally important that a housing officer contemplating issuing possession proceedings considers whether or not every effort has been made to discuss matters with the tenants, and to reach a compromise. Unless such efforts have been made, the court may well not consider it reasonable to make an order for possession.

Housing officers often do not have the authority to make the decision to issue proceedings, but are responsible for presenting the argument for commencing legal action to more senior management. The same considerations remain relevant, for the housing officer must be in a position to present all the facts of the case, in so far as they are ascertainable, so that management can take a fully informed decision.

Termination of the tenancy agreement

Once the decision has been taken to evict a tenant, it is necessary to determine (end) the tenancy. How this is done will, of course, depend on the type of tenancy. A periodic tenancy is determined by the landlord by the service of a notice to quit. However, a notice to quit has no effect on a secure or assured tenancy. Effectively, housing officers will only serve a notice to quit on tenants who do not have security of tenure, whether that is because the tenant no longer uses the dwelling as his or her only or principal home, or because the tenancy falls within one of the exceptions to security of tenure set out in Schedule 1 to either the Housing Act 1985 or the Housing Act 1988. (See further A Dymond *Security of Tenure*, chs 2 and 4, Arden's Housing Library, vol.1, 1995).

If a tenant has security of tenure, the first step towards gaining an order for possession is for the landlord to serve a notice seeking possession. A landlord can only obtain a possession order against a tenant with security of tenure under either the Housing Act 1985, or the Housing Act 1988, if the landlord is able to establish at court one of the statutory grounds for possession. Depending upon which ground is relied upon, it may also be necessary for the landlord to prove to the court that it is reasonable to make a possession order and/or that suitable alternative accommodation is available to the tenant. Many of the grounds are common to both Acts, but reference must be made to Schedule 2 to each Act. (See further A Dymond, *Security of Tenure*, chs 6 and 7, Arden's Housing Library, vol.1, 1995.) Some grounds involve proof of fault on the part of the tenant (eg rent arrears, nuisance to neighbours, deterioration of the condition of the property, breach of a term of the tenancy agreement); other grounds have a more managerial function (eg proposed works of repair by the landlord, or accommodation adapted for those with special needs when the person with those special needs no longer lives at the property).

Notice seeking possession

Where possession is sought against a secure tenant under one of the statutory grounds (which are set out in Schedule 2 to the Housing Act 1985), it will be necessary to serve a notice seeking possession. Whilst it is possible, in certain limited circumstances, for the court to dispense with the requirement that a notice seeking possession is served by an assured landlord, as a matter of good practice an assured landlord should always serve a notice seeking possession.

Commonly, housing managers or officers draft the notice seeking possession themselves, rather than seek assistance from an in-house legal department, or solicitors. The following summarises the basis of certain requirements of the notice.

A notice seeking possession must be in a prescribed form, and contain certain information, but this does not present any great difficulty, as a standard form may (and should) as a matter of good practice be used in which the relevant details may be filled in. Some landlords have their own personalised versions of the standard form. This is wholly acceptable, but there is a great risk in using any words which depart from those which have been prescribed. Housing managers should ensure that an up to date version of the form is used. An old form may vary significantly in its wording and, if used, could create considerable difficulties at trial.

Housing associations may, of course, have dealings with both secure and assured tenants. Obviously, in an individual case, it is crucial that the commencement date of the tenancy is checked, to ensure that the correct form of notice is served. In general terms, unless the tenancy falls within one of the exceptions to full security of tenure, a housing association tenancy will be assured if it was granted on or after 15 January 1989; otherwise, it will be secure.

The following five parts of the form will need completion by the housing officer:

1. The **name** of the tenant (or tenants if it is a joint tenancy).

2. The **full address** of the property for which possession is sought.

3. The **statutory grounds** on which possession is sought. All possible grounds should be included at this stage. It is not uncommon for a notice to omit a ground which could have been relied upon.

4. The **landlord's details.**

Example

Ground 1 of Schedule 2 to the Housing Act 1985 provides a ground for possession where "rent lawfully due from the tenant has not been paid or an obligation of the tenancy has been broken or not performed". An action for possession brought under Ground 2 of Schedule 2, on the basis that the tenant has caused a nuisance or annoyance to neighbours, may be supported by an action under Ground 1 (if as should be the case) the tenancy agreement includes a contractual term stipulating that the tenant must not cause a nuisance to his or her neighbours. The use of Ground 1 may be important if the contractual term is stricter than the wording of Ground 2, eg if there is a covenant against nuisance in the confines of a particularly large estate.

5. The **particulars** of each ground. In this section a summary of the facts upon which the landlord intends to rely must be included. The purpose of the notice seeking possession is to provide the tenant with sufficient details of the matters complained of to allow him or her to ensure that the situation is remedied prior to the expiry of the notice.

It is not enough merely to identify or reiterate the clauses of the tenancy agreement which have been breached. The facts which constitute the breach of tenancy agreement must be set out. Sufficient particulars have not been given if the notice merely records that the tenant is "in arrears of rent". A figure must be supplied for the arrears at the relevant date. The space provided in the standard form may well not be large enough for the details which need to be provided. It is perfectly acceptable to complete the section with "see schedule attached" and set out the full particulars on another sheet. It is important that full and proper details are provided in this section. It is better to err on the side of caution and include as many details as possible. What is included, will, of course, depend on the ground which is being relied upon.

It is also essential to ensure that the notice seeking possession has expired before proceedings are commenced. The time required depends on whether the tenancy is secure or assured, and what grounds for possession are being relied upon (see below). On the other hand, care should be taken to ensure that the notice is still in force when proceedings are commenced, because a notice seeking possession expires 12 months after it has been served. If the decision is made to initiate proceedings, but a notice has been served more than a year ago, then it is necessary to serve a new notice seeking possession.

Length of notice

All notices seeking possession under the Housing Act 1985 must specify a date before which proceedings cannot be commenced, which must not be earlier than the date upon which the tenancy could have been brought to an end by notice to quit. The same is true under the Housing Act 1988, unless the landlord is relying on grounds 1,2,5,6,7,9 or 16 of Schedule 2. The minimum period for a notice to quit is four weeks. A monthly tenancy will require a period of at least one month. The notice must expire on a day which is the last day of a period of a tenancy. (For examples of notices seeking possession, see A Dymond *Security of Tenure*, appendix, Arden's Housing Library vol.1, 1995).

Choice of court

The county court has jurisdiction to decide any action for the recovery of land (section 21(1) of the County Courts Act 1984). It is less costly to bring proceedings in the county court than in the High Court. There may be occasions when it is preferable to commence proceedings in the High Court because of the need for the greater speed of the High Court – eg an action for summary possession against squatters. It should be borne in mind that a landlord who commences proceedings in the High Court which could have been brought in the county court will not be able to recover all (or in some circumstances any) of his costs. This book generally concentrates on county court procedure because the overwhelming majority of cases in which housing managers and officers will have involvement will be in the county court.

Proceedings must be commenced in the court which has jurisdiction for the area in which the property is situated (County Court Rules 1981 (CCR), Order 4 rule 3). Accordingly, it is necessary to check that the right county court is being used, although this will rarely be a problem in practice. If proceedings are commenced in the wrong court, the judge has the power to transfer proceedings to the right court (CCR Order 16, rule 2).

Summons and pleadings

Possession actions are commenced by the landlord preparing and filing at the court a summons for possession, together with the *particulars of claim*, a formal document (or pleading) which sets out the facts upon which the landlord intends to rely and the relief to which the landlord claims to be entitled. The landlord is named in the summons as the *plaintiff*, ie the person bringing the claim. The tenant (or tenants) and any other occupiers against whom possession is sought are named in the summons as the *defendant(s)*.

Where there is more than one defendant they are numbered in the summons and in the particulars of claim as the *first defendant*, *second defendant*, and so on. The full name of each defendant should be included, and a title should be added if the gender of a defendant is unclear from the forename.

The summons includes a reply form on which the

allegations in the particulars of claim may be answered. The form does not allow for great detail, and in order fully to set out his or her case the defendant should answer the contentions pleaded in the particulars of claim in a *defence*.

In the defence the defendant should answer each allegation of fact made in the particulars of claim. The defence may *admit, not admit* or *deny* the facts relied on by the landlord and should go on to aver any other facts not mentioned in the particulars of claim, which are material to the defendant's case.

- *admit:* a fact should be admitted if it is accepted that it is true.
- *deny:* a fact should be denied if the other party knows that it is untrue.
- *not admit:* sometimes a party will not know whether or not a fact relied upon by the other is true or not. Such an allegation should be not admitted.
- *aver:* when a party wishes to rely on a fact which has not been touched upon in the other party's pleading, the fact should be averred.

Example

Sheffchester Borough Council, acting on numerous allegations from tenants in a block of flats, decide to commence possession proceedings against Mr Combes. One of the allegations against him is that he was seen vandalising the lift in the block on 2nd May 1995. In his tenancy agreement, there is an express term that the tenant must not "cause or permit any damage to the dwelling-house or the common parts of the block". The lift was repaired at considerable expense to the council. Amongst other facts relied

upon in the pleading, the council plead:
(1) the term in the tenancy agreement;
(2) that Mr Combes on 2nd May so damaged the lift that it ceased to work.

Mr Combes contends that the other tenants are lying, and trying to blame him for something he never did. The tenancy agreement does indeed include the term stated by the council, so in the defence that fact is **admitted.** He **avers** that his son can confirm that he was staying with him for two weeks in Maitland at the beginning of May 1995. In fact, by the time he returned to his home the lift had been repaired, so that he does not know anything about the incident. Accordingly, he does **not admit** that the lift was damaged on 2nd May 1995, and, even if it was damaged, he **denies** that the damage was caused by him.

If the defence raises issues which the plaintiff feels demand a response, this may be done in a *reply*. Replies are not necessary where the issues are clearly defined in the particulars of claim and the defence. It is assumed that the plaintiff denies what the defendant says in the defence. A reply is useful when the defendant raises facts which the plaintiff accepts are true. In order to save court time which would be taken up by the defendant adducing evidence about these facts, the plaintiff should admit the facts in a reply.

It is also possible for the defendant, at the same time as providing a defence, to raise a claim against the plaintiff, eg where possession is sought on the basis of rent arrears and the tenant claims that the landlord has been in breach of the covenant to keep the property in repair. Such a claim is called a *counterclaim*. A counterclaim which also amounts to a defence to the possession action is called a *set off*. The most common situation involving a set off encountered in practice is where the tenant seeks to set off damages for disrepair against rent arrears owed to the landlord. (See further A. Kilpatrick *Repairs and Maintenance,* Arden's Housing Library, vol.5, 1996).

In a case involving a counterclaim, a *reply and defence to counterclaim* must be served if the counterclaim is to be contested.

The defendant should file the defence, or defence and counterclaim, with the court within 14 days of receipt of the summons (CCR Order 9, rule 9(3)). The defendant is not precluded from filing a defence after this time limit, and even if no defence at all has been filed it is still possible for the defendant to attend the court on the return day (see below, chapter 3) and argue that there is a defence to the action (CCR Order 9, rule 9(1)). A defendant ought not to leave the defence to such a late stage as the court is likely to make the defendant pay the costs of the return date if no defence has been filed earlier.

The documents ie particulars of claim, defence, counterclaim and reply are collectively known as the pleadings in a case.

Content of summons and particulars of claim

In possession actions, unless the claim is based on forfeiture, the summons for possession of property is form N5 (see Appendix, below). The particulars of claim do not have to be in a prescribed form, unless and this is a significant exception possession is sought on the basis of rent arrears.

Rent arrears cases

Under CCR Order 6 rule 3(3), where possession of land which consists of a dwelling-house is claimed because of non-payment of rent, the particulars of claim must be in the prescribed form and must also:

(a) state the amount due at the commencement of the proceedings;

(b) give

(i) (whether in a schedule or otherwise) particulars of all the payments which have been missed altogether;

(ii) where a history of late or underpayments is relied upon, sufficient details to establish the plaintiff's case;

(c) state any previous steps which the plaintiff has taken to recover arrears of rent and, in the case of court proceedings, state

(i) the dates when the proceedings were commenced and concluded, and

(ii) the dates and terms or any orders made;

(d) give such relevant information as is known by the plaintiff about the defendant's circumstances and, in particular, whether (and, if so, what) payments on his behalf are made direct to the plaintiff by or under the Social Security Contributions and Benefits Act 1992 (ie housing benefit direct), and

(e) if the plaintiff intends as part of his case to rely on his own financial or other circumstances, give details of all relevant facts or matters.

The *prescribed* form is form N119 (see also example in Appendix below) and if the boxes in that form are correctly completed then all the information set out in (a) to (e) above will be included.

Any landlord seeking a possession order on the basis of rent arrears (Ground 1 of Schedule 2 to the Housing

Act 1985, Grounds 8, 10 and/or 11 of Schedule 2 to the Housing Act 1988) will have to use form N119. This is the case even if other grounds for possession are being relied upon; indeed, the form has room for such grounds in paragraph 3(b). The form is only to be used where arrears of rent are the ground for possession. If arrears of rent are claimed, but the claim is only a subsidiary claim and not the reason for possession being sought, form N119 should not be used. For instance, a local authority seeking possession of a property let under a private sector leasing scheme (paragraph 6 of Schedule 1 to the Housing Act 1985) need not use form N119 simply because arrears of rent are also claimed in the action.

Much of the required information is self-explanatory. The information concerning the arrears is easily provided by a copy of the rent account, which may be attached to the form. Note that it must be an up-to-date rent account, identifying the position as at the commencement of proceedings. Other significant items for housing officers to prepare are a record of previous steps to recover the arrears of rent and the information about the tenant's circumstances.

Information about the tenant's circumstances is required because it will be necessary (except in the case of Ground 8 under the Housing Act 1988) for the landlord to show that it is reasonable for a possession order to be made. The tenant's financial position is significant, as it indicates whether the arrears have accrued because of wilful default or because of difficulties arising through circumstances beyond the tenant's control (eg illness, recent unemployment, or difficulties encountered with housing benefit). With regard to earlier steps to recover the arrears, the court will wish to know whether or not the tenant has been co-operative in suggesting payment of the arrears, and whether or not any agreement was reached, and, if so, whether or not the tenant kept to the agreement.

The parties

Obviously, the parties to a possession action will normally be the landlord and the tenant. If the tenancy is a joint tenancy, all the joint tenants (whether or not they all still reside in the property) must be joined as parties to the action.

In certain types of possession action persons who are not named in the tenancy agreement will have to be joined. In a case where the tenant has left, but the tenant's lodgers or friends still reside in the property, possession will be sought against the occupiers. However, it may also be necessary to join the tenant as a party if he or she owes arrears of rent.

Other parties may join the action at a later stage, or be joined, if it appears that the landlord needs to bring action against a new party. A person not initially named by the landlord in the summons (eg a non-tenant spouse) may join the action if he or she claims to have a right to remain in the property.

CHAPTER 2

WHAT NEEDS TO BE PROVED?

Ownership of the land / *Proving the tenancy agreement* / **Termination of tenants' interest** / *Form of the notice* / *Service of the notice* / **Reason for seeking possession** / *Non-secure and assured tenants* / *Secure or assured tenants* / *Reasonableness* / *Suitable alternative accommodation* / **Money judgments** / **Checklists** / *Loss of security of tenure* / *Death of tenant* / *Notice to quit by joint tenant* / *Exceptions to security of tenure* / *Claims based on statutory grounds for possession*

The evidence required in each case will vary, and more detailed considerations of the evidence which is required in certain types of case commonly encountered by housing managers are provided in Part III. In this chapter, first factors which are common to all possession actions are considered and secondly checklists are provided as guides to individual types of claim.

In general terms, in any possession action the landlord must prove:

1. ownership of the land
2. termination of the tenant's interest
3. reasons for seeking possession

Ownership of the land

The landlord's title (ownership) to the property must be proved. This is rarely a problem in residential possession actions, where it will be sufficient to prove the tenancy agreement.

Proving the tenancy agreement

If there is a written tenancy agreement, then the original tenancy agreement is required at court for proof of title (and should be at court for its terms and conditions in any event). As a matter of good practice, the original agreement should always be available at court. If the original tenancy agreement has been lost then a copy will normally be accepted as sufficient proof.

If no copy of the agreement can be found then it will be necessary to establish the agreement in some other way. If the defendant attends court there will be little difficulty, as he or she will accept that there is an agreement. If the tenant does not attend, the landlord is in the difficult position of having to prove the written agreement without being able to provide the court with a copy of it. Since, however, a tenancy need not be in writing, proof of payment and acceptance of rent is sufficient to show an agreement for a tenancy between the parties. Accordingly, as a last resort, a copy of the rent account which bears the tenant's name, the address of the property and which shows payments being made may be used as proof of title.

Termination of the tenant's interest

Proof must be provided that the tenant's interest in the property has been determined (possibly by surrender, but more usually by the service of a notice to quit), or, if the tenant has security of tenure under the Housing Act 1985, or Housing Act 1988, that a notice seeking possession has been served. Essentially, this element concerns proof that a notice in the correct form has been served. This element accordingly divides into two factors:

- the form of the notice
- service of the notice on the tenant.

Form of the notice

Housing officers usually use a standard form. As long as the correct form has been used, and has been completed properly, there will be no difficulty in proving the first of these factors. A true copy of the notice which was served is simply provided to the court. (See further chapter 1, above).

Service of the notice

Where reliance is being placed on a notice to quit or a notice seeking possession, the landlord must prove that the notice has been served on the tenant. Section 83(1) of the Housing Act 1985 states that the court will not entertain proceedings for possession of a dwelling let under a secure tenancy unless the landlord has "served on the tenant" a notice seeking possession in the prescribed form.

Under section 8 of the Housing Act 1988, proof of service of a notice seeking possession is also required unless "the court considers it is just and equitable to dispense with the requirement of such a notice"(section 8(1)(b)). This power to dispense with the requirement of a notice seeking possession cannot be used if the landlord is seeking possession under ground 8 of Schedule 2 to the Housing Act 1988 (ie the mandatory ground for rent arrears). As a matter of good practice, a notice seeking possession should always be served.

Physically serving the notice

The best way to serve a notice is to visit the tenant and hand it to him or her personally. Personal service removes any doubts as to whether or not the notice was received. It also allows the opportunity for the housing officer to discuss the case with the tenant and explain the importance of the notice, the consequences of a possession order (advice to the tenant as to his or her rights as a homeless person, if relevant), or else see if some form of compromise can be made, eg an arrangement for the payment of rent arrears, if that is the ground for possession.

In order to avoid subsequent disputes as to whether or not the notice was duly served, or when it was served, most notices will bear a memorandum of service and the housing officer should ensure that the tenant signs and dates the memorandum on the landlord's copy of the notice.

Although this is the best form of service, personal service is not essential or indeed in certain circumstances even possible, eg where the tenant has permanently abandoned the property and the landlord is unaware of the tenant's whereabouts.

If the tenancy is in writing, the landlord will normally be aided by section 146 of the Law of Property Act 1925. The housing officer may serve the notice by leaving it at the tenant's last known place of abode or business in the United Kingdom. Alternatively, the officer may send the notice by registered post or recorded delivery addressed to the tenant's last known place of abode or business.

If such methods of service are used then the tenant will be deemed to have been served with the notice, and it will not be necessary for the landlord to show that the tenant actually received it. This method of service is only available where the tenancy agreement itself has a term permitting such service. Social landlords normally include such a term in their agreements, and if the point arises at trial, it is only necessary to direct the judge to the agreement itself or a copy of the standard terms and conditions used.

Deceased tenants

If the tenant has died, and there is no-one entitled to the tenancy, the notice to quit must now be served on the Public Trustee. (Before 1 July 1995, service had to be on the President of the Family Division.)

Reason for seeking possession

Non-secure/assured tenants

If possession is sought against a tenant who falls within one of the exceptions to the security of tenure provided by the Housing Act 1988, or the Housing Act 1985, then it will only be necessary to demonstrate to the court:

- the facts which show that the tenancy falls within one of the exceptions to security of tenure, and
- that the tenancy has been properly determined.

If these factors are proved then the court must order possession. Similarly, if it is shown that the tenant has abandoned the property then it will only be necessary to show that the contractual tenancy has been determined for the landlord to demonstrate that he has a right to possession.

Secure/assured tenants

If the tenant has security of tenure, then, of course, it will be necessary to prove that at least one of the statutory grounds for possession is made out. Depending on which ground is relied upon, it may also be necessary to show that it is reasonable for the court to grant an order for possession and/or that suitable alternative accommodation is available to the tenant.

Reasonableness

Where a social landlord is seeking possession pursuant to Grounds 1 to 8, or 12 to 16 of the Housing Act 1985, or Grounds 9 to 16 of the Housing Act 1988, it will have to demonstrate to the court that it is reasonable to make an order for possession.

When the case is based on one of these discretionary grounds for possession, the court must explicitly address the question of reasonableness in its judgment or that decision will be open to appeal. The question of reasonableness is one of fact and degree, and it will be rare for a judge's finding on reasonableness to be interfered with on appeal.

The factors which are relevant to the issue of reasonableness naturally vary according to the ground relied upon by the landlord. In general terms, it is a question of weighing up the hardship to the landlord if a possession order were not granted against the hardship to the tenant if it were.

Tenant's circumstances

The tenant's personal circumstances and those of the people living with the tenant are considered by the court. These will include:

- the age of the occupiers;
- whether or not the occupiers are employed;
- whether or not children live in the property;
- the occupier's health;
- how long the occupiers have resided at the property.

Circumstances of the landlord

Where the landlord is an individual, the factors which are taken into account by the court are similar to those affecting the tenant. For example, the court may be faced with the difficult balance of weighing up the hardship to an elderly landlord who seeks to return to live in a property and who cannot afford high arrears of rent, against the hardship to a tenant who has recently lost his or her job who has children to support.

Obviously, very different considerations apply when a social landlord seeks possession. It is the function of public authorities and housing associations to provide housing to those in most need of it. That, however, does not mean that their tenants may be allowed to take advantage of the situation. A social landlord has to take into account the interests of its other tenants (eg in a possession action based upon nuisance to neighbours) and to those who are awaiting housing.

Case report

Mr Bistram was a secure tenant of the Woking District Council. The main complaint of his neighbours, both those who lived in the same block of flats and those who lived opposite, was his use of threats and foul language. The judge found that the conduct was still continuing "as far as that is relevant" but decided that bad language was "no doubt very much a common experience in certain areas," and refused to order possession. The Council appealed successfully. One of the factors which the Court of Appeal took into account was that the judge had not referred in his judgment to the authority's obligation to the other tenants on the estate and the interests of those tenants. These were relevant to the decision, and should have been taken into account by the judge.
Woking Borough Council v Bistram (1993) 27 HLR 1, CA.

Suitable alternative accommodation

A landlord seeking possession under Grounds 9 to 16 of the Housing Act 1985 must demonstrate that suitable alternative accommodation is available for the tenant. The availability of suitable alternative accommodation is itself a ground for possession under the Housing Act 1988 (Ground 9). Part IV of Schedule 2 to the Housing Act 1985 sets out certain requirements concerning the suitability of the proposed alternative accommodation. A similar list of requirements appears in Part III of Schedule 2 to the Housing Act 1988. (See further A. Dymond *Security of Tenure*, ch 8, Arden's Housing Library, vol 1, 1995).

Local authority tenants

Where a local authority is seeking to show that the proposed alternative accommodation is suitable it must satisfy the court as to two main points:

- that the tenant will have a tenancy of similar security of tenure (eg a secure or assured tenancy).
- that the property is suitable to the tenant's needs.

The second factor includes a number of points which must be addressed in the preparation of evidence for the trial.

Although the list that follows is not exhaustive, it consists of the main points which must be addressed in deciding what is suitable alternative accommodation.

1. The nature of the accommodation which it is the practice of the landlord to allocate to persons with similar needs. This is the most significant factor. The local authority will need a witness to provide details of its allocation policy showing the size and type of property which it would let to a tenant of the same type. The defendant's main objections to proposed accommodation is that it is too small, or on too high a floor, because the tenant is elderly, or in poor health, or is concerned about the safety of children. These complaints may be answered by showing that the property offered meets

the local authority's policy in this regard.
2. The distance of the accommodation from the place of work or education of the tenant and the members of the tenant's family.
3. The distance from the home of any member of the tenant's family if proximity to it is essential to that person's or the tenant's well-being.
4. The terms on which the accommodation is available.
5. If furniture was provided by the landlord for use under the secure tenancy, whether furniture is to be provided in the other accommodation and the nature of that furniture.

Landlords who are not local authorities

Where the landlord is not a local authority, a certificate from the local authority that suitable alternative accommodation will be provided by the local authority will be conclusive evidence that the proposed alternative accommodation is suitable.

If the landlord is unable to rely on such a certificate, it will be necessary to demonstrate to the court that the landlord or another landlord is able to make a suitable property available.

The tenant must be given similar security of tenure (generally an assured tenancy, but not an assured shorthold tenancy or an assured tenancy which is subject to one of the mandatory grounds for possession under grounds 1 to 5 of the Housing Act 1988). Otherwise, if the tenancy is a secure tenancy then the considerations set out above will apply.

Where the tenancy is an assured tenancy, Part III of Schedule 2 to the Housing Act 1988 requires that the proposed alternative accommodation is:

- reasonably suitable to the needs of the tenant and their family as regards proximity to place of work; and either
- similar, in terms of rental and extent, to the accommodation afforded by such a dwelling-house as would be provided in the neighbourhood by any housing authority for persons whose needs as regards extent are – in the opinion of the court – similar to those of the tenant and his or her family; or
- reasonably suitable to the means of the tenant and to the needs of the tenant and his or her family as regards extent and character.

The requirements make specific comparison with the sort of property the tenant could expect to receive from a local authority. As in cases brought by local authority landlords, the crucial evidence will normally be that of the authority's allocation policy.

Money judgments

In many possession proceedings, the landlord will be seeking not only possession but also some form of money judgment against the tenant or other occupiers of the property. This, obviously, goes without saying in an action based upon rent arrears, but in preparing a case based on other grounds, housing officers should always check the position of the rent account.

A tenant without security of tenure, whose tenancy has been brought to an end is in law a trespasser, and damages for use and occupation may be sought against him or her. Such damages are usually referred to as *mesne profits*.

Some time will elapse between the date of the possession order and the day upon which possession is actually delivered up. Possession orders are commonly suspended for a period of time and, even if an immediate order for possession is granted, if the occupier does not quit the premises it will be necessary for the landlord to obtain an appointment with the bailiffs for the order to be enforced which will cause some delay. Compensation for this period of occupation is also available to the landlord.

Checklists

The following are simple checklists which set out the basic elements required to establish the right to possession in some of the more commonly encountered types of case.

Loss of security of tenure

A tenant only has security of tenure if he or she occupies the dwelling house as his or her only or principal home (section 81 of the Housing Act 1985; section 1 of the Housing Act 1988). If the tenant ceases so to do, then possession may be gained if it can be shown that the contractual tenancy has been determined (by notice to quit or surrender). This topic is considered in more detail in chapter 8.

CHECK – the tenancy agreement with the contractual tenant.

CHECK – evidence that the contractual tenant is no longer residing in the premises as the principal home.

CHECK – service of notice to quit in prescribed form.

CHECK – rent account for any arrears of rent up to the expiry of the notice to quit (and to show contractual rent at time of expiry).
CHECK – calculation of damages for use and occupation against any trespasser in the premises (based on the rent which would have been received by the landlord if the premises had been let under a tenancy).

Death of tenant
If the tenant has died, different considerations apply. If the tenancy, whether secure or assured, is a joint tenancy, then the remaining tenant, or tenants, remain as secure or assured tenants. Where a sole tenant dies, there may be questions of succession to be considered. (For a full discussion of who is entitled to succeed to a secure or an assured tenancy see C. Hunter *Tenants' Rights,* Arden's Housing Library vol 2, 1995).
CHECK – the tenancy agreement.
CHECK – proof of the death of the tenant (death certificate).
CHECK – evidence of service of notice to quit (now on Public Trustee – before 1 July 1995 on the President of the Family Division).
CHECK – evidence showing persons in occupation are not entitled to succeed to the tenancy.

Notice to quit by joint tenant
This is particularly relevant to cases involving the breakdown of relationships. (See A. Dymond, *Security of Tenure,* ch 12, Arden's Housing Library, vol 1, 1995)
CHECK – joint tenancy agreement.
CHECK – notice to quit in correct form served on the landlord.

CHECK – rent account in order to prove any rent arrears against both joint tenants, and to show calculation of mesne profits to be claimed against the remaining occupier after expiry of notice to quit.

Exceptions to security of tenure

Schedule 1 to the Housing Act 1985 and Schedule 1 to the Housing Act 1988 set out those tenancies which do not have the security of tenure provided by those Acts. Some of the particular exceptions are considered below. In general terms, the landlord must establish that the exception applies and then show that the contractual tenancy has been determined.

Tied accommodation

Service occupiers do not have security of tenure under the Housing Act 1988 because they are licensees and only tenants have security of tenure under the 1988 Act. Licensees do have security of tenure under the Housing Act 1985, but paragraph 2 of Schedule 1 to the 1985 Act precludes service occupiers from having security of tenure. Effectively, both secure and assured landlords need to demonstrate the same factors to succeed in obtaining possession against an alleged service occupier.

CHECK – the contract of employment.

This is crucial, as it is the basis of establishing that the exception to security of tenure applies. The contract of employment should contain a term under which the employee is required to occupy the dwelling-house for the better performance of his or her duties. If the contract does not require the employee to occupy the premises, then the employer will have to provide evidence that it was **necessary** for the employee to live in the accommodation provided by the employer. A resident caretaker responsible for the running of a housing estate or school is an obvious example. The contract itself may provide strong indications that it was necessary for the employee to reside in the property, by listing duties of the employee which may show that the job could only be carried out with the employee in occupation, eg an estate caretaker may be required to be on call 24 hours a day to deal with any emergencies on the estate. If this is not the case, then evidence will have to be given of the nature of the job, usually by the relevant member of the employer's personnel department.

One significant question which should be addressed in preparation is: "would the employee have been taken on if, at the time he or she applied for the job, the employee had made it clear that she would not have been prepared to reside in the accommodation provided?" If the answer to this question is Yes, then it is unlikely that the court would find that it was necessary for the employee to reside in the property.

CHECK – the employment has been determined. This will vary according to each contract of employment and may be proved by producing the letter of notice. Of course, the notice period must have expired before the proceedings can be issued.

Development land: short-life user property

Premises on land acquired for development which is being used pending development for temporary housing are excluded under paragraph 3 of Schedule 1 to the Housing Act 1985. Such property is often referred to as "short-life". When possession is sought against

non-secure tenants of this type, the following evidence is required.
CHECK – the tenancy or licence agreement.
CHECK – evidence that the land on which the dwelling stands is being used pending development. The landlord may not be the body which will be carrying out the development, but detailed evidence will be required of the nature of the works proposed and the fact that the plans for development are to go ahead, this may include planning consents.
CHECK – copy of the notice to quit in prescribed form and proof of service.
CHECK – rent account for any rent arrears and mesne profits.

Subleasing schemes

Where tenancies are non-secure due to paragraph 6 of Schedule 1 to the Housing Act 1985 the following evidence is required.
CHECK – lease made between the owner of the property and the local authority. This proves that the authority have title. It should also contain certain clauses which are essential to prove that the exception applies in the case, namely:
CHECK – a clause specifying that the property is to be used for the provision of temporary housing accommodation.
CHECK – a fixed term for the lease or a clause providing that the authority will give up vacant possession of the property when required to do so by the lessor.

It should be noted that a fixed term lease, unlike a periodic tenancy, will almost certainly attract stamp duty unless the rent for the property is very low. It is important to check that the lease which is to be produced to the court bears stamp duty, for otherwise the court will not allow it as evidence (section 14 of the Stamp Act 1891).

CHECK – the non-secure tenancy agreement. This proves the authority's title against the occupier. Note that the terms of the agreement may be significant, as some authorities include terms in their non-secure tenancy agreements which impose restrictions on when possession may be sought, eg when there are arrears of rent or when the owner of the property requires vacant possession. Accordingly, it may be necessary to ensure that evidence is available to show that one of the conditions included in the agreement has been fulfilled.

CHECK – copy notice to quit and proof of service.

CHECK – evidence of rent arrears, and mesne profits.

Claims based on statutory grounds for possession

Rent Arrears: Ground 1 of the 1985 Act

For a full discussion of this topic relating to secure tenants, see chapter 7.

CHECK – tenancy agreement.

CHECK – notice seeking possession in prescribed form and proof of service.

CHECK – rent account showing the current rent and the full history of arrears. For the purposes of showing the ground applies the account must show arrears as of the date of the issue of proceedings (date of summons).

CHECK – reasonableness, eg level of arrears, efforts by tenant to pay off arrears, any agreements made with the tenant which have subsequently been breached.

Rent arrears: Ground 8 of the 1988 Act

For a full discussion of this topic relating to assured tenants, see chapter 7.

CHECK – tenancy agreement (note the period of the tenancy).

CHECK – notice seeking possession in prescribed form and proof of service.

CHECK – rent account showing the current rent and the full history of the arrears. The requirements of the ground vary as to the period of the tenancy.

CHECK – weekly or fortnightly tenancy: landlord must show both at the date of service of the notice seeking possession and at the date of the hearing of the action, rent arrears of at least 13 weeks rent.

CHECK – monthly tenancy: landlord must show both at the date of service of the notice seeking possession and at the date of the hearing of the action, rent arrears of at least three months' rent.

Rent arrears: Ground 10 of the 1988 Act

For a full discussion of this topic relating to assured tenant, see chapter 7.

CHECK – tenancy agreement.

CHECK – notice seeking possession in prescribed form and proof of service.

CHECK – rent account showing current rent and full history of arrears. For the ground to be made out, the account must show that the tenant was in arrears both at the date on which the proceedings were begun (date of issue of summons) and at the date of the service of the notice seeking possession.

CHECK – reasonableness, eg level of arrears, efforts by

tenant to pay off arrears, any agreements made with the tenant which have subsequently been breached.

Nuisance and annoyance to neighbours

Possession may be claimed for nuisance and annoyance to neighbours under Ground 2 of Schedule 2 to the 1985 Act or Ground 14 of Schedule 2 to the 1988 Act. For a full discussion of nuisance cases see chapter 8.
CHECK – tenancy agreement (note any covenants against nuisance and annoyance).
CHECK – notice seeking possession in the prescribed form and proof of service of notice.
CHECK – evidence from neighbours that they have suffered a nuisance caused by the tenant or someone else residing in the dwelling, **OR**
CHECK – proof that the tenant has been convicted of using or allowing the dwelling to be used for immoral or illegal purposes (certificate signed by the clerk of the court giving the substance and effect of the conviction).
CHECK – evidence about reasonableness. This is made up in part by the evidence of the tenants as to the severity of the nuisance and whether or not it has abated and in part by the evidence of the housing officer with conduct of the case. The housing officer needs to provide evidence of the complaints made to him, meetings with the defendant, the defendant's reactions and any other steps taken.

Deterioration of premises

Grounds 3 and 4 of Schedule 2 to the Housing Act 1985, or Ground 13 and 15 of Schedule 2 to the Housing Act 1988.
CHECK – tenancy agreement (note any covenant

regarding waste, or neglect, or tenant-like behaviour, by tenant).
CHECK – notice seeking possession in prescribed form and proof of service.
CHECK – evidence that the condition of dwelling, the common parts or the furniture have deteriorated (photographs needed).
CHECK – evidence that the deterioration was caused by the tenant (or person residing with the tenant).
CHECK – evidence as to reasonableness, eg, efforts, or proposals, by the tenant to remedy the deterioration. If the tenant is vulnerable and unable to cope with looking after the property, evidence should be obtained from social services.

Accommodation pending works
Ground 8 of Schedule 2 to the Housing Act 1985.
CHECK – tenancy agreement.
CHECK – notice seeking possession in prescribed form and proof of service.
CHECK – evidence from the housing officer who organised the letting that the dwelling was made available for occupation by the tenant (or a predecessor) while works were being carried out on the dwelling which the tenant previously occupied as his or her only principal home.
CHECK – tenancy agreement for previous dwelling showing that tenant was a secure tenant of that dwelling.
CHECK – evidence that the tenant (or a predecessor) accepted the tenancy of the dwelling of which possession is sought on the understanding that the tenant would give up occupation when, on completion of the

works, the other dwelling-house was again available for occupation under a secure tenancy.
CHECK – proof that the works have now been completed and the other dwelling is available.
CHECK – evidence as to reasonableness, eg the reason for undertaking the works, the length of time the works have taken as opposed to how long the tenant was told the works would take.

Landlord's works

Grounds 10 and 10A of Schedule 2 to the Housing Act 1985.
CHECK – tenancy agreement.
CHECK – notice seeking possession in prescribed form and proof of service.
CHECK – if the landlord intends to do the works, evidence from surveyor of the landlord's plans to demolish or reconstruct the building or part of the building which includes the dwelling, **OR** that works are planned to the building, and (in any event) evidence that the works cannot reasonably be done without vacant possession of the dwelling.
CHECK – if the works are to be done by another body evidence is required of an intention to sell the premises with vacant possession within a reasonable time of obtaining possession and evidence that the property (or part of it) is in an approved development area.
CHECK – suitability of proposed alternative accommodation.

Accommodation required for employees:

Ground 12 of Schedule 2 to the Housing Act 1985.
CHECK – evidence (including plans) that the dwelling

forms part of, or is in the grounds of, a non-housing building, or in the grounds of a cemetery.
CHECK – contract of employment of the tenant, and evidence from personnel department that the property was let to the tenant in consequence of employment.
CHECK – evidence that the dwelling is now required for a new employee.
CHECK – evidence concerning suitability of proposed alternative accommodation.
CHECK – any further evidence as to issue of reasonableness.

Accommodation required for employees: Ground 16 of Schedule 2 to the Housing Act 1988.
CHECK – tenancy agreement.
CHECK – contract of employment with the tenant.
CHECK – evidence that the tenancy was granted to the tenant in consequence of the tenant's employment by the landlord seeking possession or by a previous landlord under the tenancy.
CHECK – proof of termination of employment.
CHECK – evidence as to issue of reasonableness.

Under-occupation:
Ground 16 of Schedule 2 to the Housing Act 1985.
CHECK – tenancy agreement granted to former, deceased tenant.
CHECK – proof that former tenant deceased (death certificate).
CHECK – tenancy agreement with current tenant as successor (must not be spouse of former tenant for ground to apply).
CHECK – notice seeking possession in the prescribed

form and proof of service (must have been served no earlier than six months after the death of the tenant, and no later than 12 months after the death).
CHECK – evidence that dwelling is more extensive than is reasonably required by the successor.
CHECK – suitability of proposed alternative accommodation.
CHECK – any further evidence as to reasonableness.

CHAPTER 3

THE RETURN DATE

Nature of the hearing / ***Defences raised at return date*** / ***Typical outcomes at return date*** / **Proving the case** / ***Adjournments*** / ***Consolidation***

All possession actions initially come to court for a brief hearing referred to as the "return date". This chapter deals with the purpose, and nature, of this hearing.

The nature of the hearing

A possession action is commenced by the issue in the relevant county court of a summons, referred to as a fixed date summons by the landlord against the tenant or occupier. It is called a *fixed date summons* because the summons bears a date upon which the parties must attend the court for the hearing of the action: *the return date* (see Appendix, below). The date is allocated by the court. The case is then listed, usually with a number of other possession actions. Most courts operate a system whereby all possession actions are listed on a particular morning or afternoon. This is called the *possession list*.

Some courts set aside a morning or afternoon specifically for possession actions brought by social landlords, or sometimes even one such landlord.

The possession list takes place in *open court*, ie the public have access to the court, and legal representatives have to wear the appropriate court clothing. It is usual for the list to be divided into blocks of cases all of which are listed for a particular time. Thus, although the summons may say that the case is listed for 11 o'clock, in reality it will be one of around a dozen or more cases all listed for this time, which will be heard during the following hour. (It is not unheard of for thirty cases to be listed for an hour.) The court usher will announce all the cases in the list shortly before the time stated and all the parties have to go into court at that point. The case will probably not be announced again and if the case is called on and the plaintiff is not present the claim for possession will be dismissed.

Defences raised at return date

As the number of cases allocated to one list indicates, only a few minutes will be allotted to one case. If the defendant has some form of arguable defence then the case will almost certainly not be contested that day, unless the point in issue is a very minor one. In theory, the defendant should have completed the reply form which is attached to the summons and returned this to the court indicating what his or her defence to the action is. It is important to check whether or not such a reply has been received. The tenant may, of course, have already taken legal advice and a full defence may have been filed. In such cases, it usual for the parties to agree directions as to the future conduct of the case and to write to the court requesting that the return date be vacated and that the judge make an order in the terms of the agreed directions.

If there has not been enough time to do this, it is proper for one of the parties to attend to make such an application. There is, however, nothing to prevent a defendant turning up at court on the return date and seeking to argue that there is a defence to the action; indeed, the rules of the court allow this (CCR Order 9 rule 9(3)).

Typical outcomes at return date

Assuming that the hearing has not been vacated (ie both parties agree that it is not necessary) because the parties have agreed directions for the future conduct of the case, the following may happen at the return date:

1. The landlord does not attend. The case will almost certainly be dismissed, and, if the tenant has attended, the landlord will be ordered to pay the defendant's costs.

2. The defendant does not attend. The landlord will be asked formally to present its case and seek an order.

3. The defendant does attend but admits that he or she does not have a defence to the action for possession. The landlord will be asked formally to present its case and seek an order. The defendant will be allowed to ask questions of the landlord's witnesses, if any matters are not agreed, and the landlord's representative will in turn have the opportunity of questioning the defendant. Even where the tenant agrees to the order the court must examine the facts. On consent orders, see further chapter 10.

4. The defendant attends, either with representation or in person, and demonstrates that he or she has an arguable defence to the action. The case will normally then be adjourned and directions given by the judge for the future conduct of the case.

Proving the case

There is a tendency for the return date to be viewed as a somewhat informal hearing. This is because of the nature of the possession list. A large number of parties will be present and often tenants will be appearing in person. Additionally, there is a need to deal with the actions swiftly in order to get through the whole list.

It must be emphasised that housing managers and officers should not view the return date as an informal hearing. All the court rules with regard to evidence apply and the hearing is a trial, albeit a brief one. The judge or district judge will wish to deal with the matter quickly, but no corners will be cut. This means that a housing officer, when giving evidence or presenting a case must have all the essential information and documentation to hand.

A local authority or housing association will regularly be appearing before the same judge at possession lists. Indeed, the judge's view of the landlord will be significantly coloured by how such routine possession actions are presented. Thus, the presentation of a possession action may impact not only on other claims for possession but also on other litigation being conducted by the landlord. It is accordingly vital to demonstrate the authority's or association's efficiency and fairness at such hearings.

Assuming the tenant does not have a defence to the

action, the landlord will have formally to prove its case. This is so even if the tenant has admitted the landlord's right to possession on the reply attached to the summons and even if he or she does not attend the hearing. The officer, whether presenting the case in person or appearing as a witness, takes the stand and gives evidence on oath and refers the judge to any evidence which may have been given by affidavit. Each element required to be proved is put to the judge, who may ask questions of the officer. Any relevant documents are handed to the judge for his or her inspection. The terms of the order sought are then put to the court. The judge will then make an order, depending upon whether or not the court is satisfied that the case is proved.

Adjournments

There will be occasions when it will not be possible for a case to be heard on the return date. The reason for the need to adjourn the matter until another day may be the fault of the landlord or the defendant.

Inability to prove case

If the landlord is unable to present its case, eg because a witness cannot attend, it will be necessary to apply for an adjournment. Ideally, this should be done by writing to the court before the return date itself. If the defendant is represented, every attempt should be made to agree such an adjournment in advance.

If the reason for the proposed adjournment is the lack of a witness, although evidence must usually be oral there is provision for use of affidavit evidence and, if the need is realised at an early enough stage, it may be possible to avoid an adjournment by the use of affidavit evidence. Thus, in a rent arrears case, if someone is in the position to give the details of the arrears owed, or of any discussions between the parties, but the person who served the notice seeking possession is unavailable, it may be possible to prove the service of the notice seeking possession by the use of an affidavit.

As to the consequences of being unable to prove the case, see the decision in *Lambeth LBC v White*, below p67.

Change of circumstances before return date

Sometimes the landlord will ask for an adjournment not because of procedural difficulties but because the reason for commencing proceedings no longer exists. An obvious example is if the tenant has paid a large sum off the rent arrears shortly before the hearing to the extent that it would no longer be reasonable for an order for possession to be made. Another example arises in private sector leasing accommodation. Often, possession proceedings are commenced on the basis that the head lease is about to expire. Subsequently, it transpires that the owner is willing to enter into a new lease with the local authority. Possession proceedings may be adjourned pending the outcome of negotiations for a new lease. The court will almost invariably be willing to adjourn proceedings on the basis that the matter may well be settled in the future.

In some circumstances it may be more appropriate to withdraw the case altogether, eg the arrears have been completely paid off, or negotiations regarding a lease have been successfully completed. While it is always open to a plaintiff to withdraw his or her case, the consequence is that the costs of the case cannot be recovered. In cases of arrears it may be appropriate to proceed to the return date in order to obtain an order for costs against the tenant, if nothing else. Careful consideration should be given, however, to whether seeking such an order is appropriate where tenants are struggling with debt problems and – having made the effort to clear the rent arrears – are nonetheless faced with a further debt.

Court's attitude to request

An adjournment will usually be granted to the landlord unless the need for the adjournment is attributable to inefficiency. Accordingly, the court will wish to be provided with (detailed) reasons for the failure of a witness to attend.

If it appears to a housing officer at court that another case brought by his or her employer has been listed, but that no officer is in attendance for that case, the officer should contact the department to ascertain why this is the case. It may be that there is correspondence before the court requesting an adjournment or withdrawing a case, but if not, and the absence of a representative is inexplicable, it is quite proper for the officer to ask to address the court. Having apologised, ask that the matter be "adjourned generally, liberty to restore".

Defence raised

If the defendant attends and it appears to the court that there is an arguable defence to the possession action, then an adjournment will normally be granted. It should be noted that it is possible to adjourn part of an action only. Thus, in a case where there is no defence to the claim for possession but there is a dispute over the money claim for arrears, it may be appropriate to ask for the money claim to be adjourned with liberty to restore.

It will rarely be possible for the landlord to oppose the defendant's first application for an adjournment (although any subsequent requests for adjournments should be carefully evaluated), if it appears to the court that the defendant has some form of defence. Nevertheless, if the landlord has received no indication that such a request would be made, the landlord is perfectly entitled to ask for the costs of the return date "in any event". Thus, even if the landlord subsequently loses the trial of the action, at least the costs of the return date will be borne by the defendant.

On such an adjournment, there will be directions as to the procedural steps which need to be taken at trial. Chapter 4 sets out the normal steps which should be requested, and explains their significance. Court proceedings take a notoriously long time to reach completion, although the situation has improved in recent years. If at all possible the landlord will wish the matter to proceed as quickly as possible. At the return date, if a defence to the action has not been filed, it may be useful to ask the judge to consider making an *unless order* (see further chapter 4).

Consolidation

It is possible that a landlord may wish to bring possession proceedings when there is already a claim being brought against the landlord by the tenant. The most common example arises when the tenant has made a claim for damages for disrepair against the landlord. The landlord may wish to bring proceedings for possession. How this is dealt with procedurally depends upon whether there is any connection between the reason for wishing to bring possession proceedings, and the nature of the tenant's claim. If there is no connection, the possession action should be commenced and remain a separate action, but if a common question of fact or law arises the two actions may be consolidated under CCR Order 13, rule 9.

Example

Mr and Mrs Legg have a secure tenancy of a council flat. They have commenced an action for damages for disrepair against their landlord Millbury Borough Council. In addition, because of the disrepair, the Leggs have refused to pay any rent and arrears are now £3,650. Millbury Borough Council accept that there has been some disrepair at the property, but the repairs have now been carried out and it is unlikely that the Leggs would obtain more than £1,500 in damages at trial. The council have issued possession proceedings based on arrears of rent. This is a case where it is appropriate for the two cases to be consolidated.

CHAPTER 4

PRETRIAL PROCEDURE

Directions: generally / Procedural steps / *Pleadings / Discovery / Witness statements* / Unless orders / Typical Directions

Where the possession action is not dispensed with at the return date, generally because it is going to be defended, then a number of procedural steps may take place prior to the trial. Such steps are covered by what are known as *directions*. This chapter considers the various mandatory procedural steps which have to take place before a full trial, and other optional measures which may assist in the conduct of a case or even remove the need for a trial.

County court litigation is run in accordance with rules which are set out in the County Court Rules (CCR). The procedure which is provided for the preparation for trial is designed to ensure that both parties should have every opportunity to bring the matter to a swift conclusion. The process of pleadings ensures that each side knows the other's basic case. If the pleadings do not make this clear, the party can be asked to clarify the position.

Each side must provide the other with the documents they have relating to the case. Before trial, both parties must provide witness statements containing the evidence which will be given at trial. Accordingly, there is a process by which each party is well aware of the other's contentions well before trial. This encourages settlement and also serves to narrow the issues between the parties which will be in dispute at trial, reducing the amount of court time which will have to be set aside should a trial be necessary. The procedural rules should ensure fairness towards the parties, in that neither side should be in a position to take the other by surprise at the trial.

The finer points of procedure can be very complicated and housing managers or officers do not need detailed understanding of the various tactical nuances. It is, however, important to have some knowledge, as it will be housing officers who will be gathering evidence, and who will need to provide the information which allows legal representatives to comply with the procedure and to enable housing officers to make a more positive contribution to cases, eg suggesting tactics to their lawyers.

Directions: generally

In order to ensure that the procedural steps are carried out, the court – either on the return date or at a later hearing – will issue a set of *directions* to govern the time limits in which these steps must be carried out. These directions may be agreed by the parties (in which case they will simply be rubber-stamped by the court) or may require argument in front of the judge. Where the original directions do not encompass steps which subsequently seem necessary, then an order for that direction should be sought from the court, preferably with the consent of the other side.

Procedural steps

Normally the procedural steps before trial will consist of:

1. Pleadings.
2. Discovery.
3. Witness statements.

Pleadings

Pleadings have already been considered in chapter 1. They are the formal statement of each party's case. Any pleading which leaves matters unclear may be attacked by the other party.

Further and Better Particulars

One way of seeking further information on the other side's pleadings is by asking for *further and better particulars* of a pleading.

> *Example*
>
> Bradcastle Borough Council are bringing a possession action against Mr Best, who the council say is an unlawful occupier of a council flat which had been let to Mr Groom. Mr Groom is the first defendant, and Mr Best the second defendant to the action. Mr Best has filed a defence. At paragraph 4 he states :
>
> "It is denied that the second defendant is a tres-

passer. The second defendant avers that the first defendant left the premises and informed the plaintiff that he was leaving, and asked the plaintiff to transfer the tenancy to the second defendant. In full knowledge that the first defendant had abandoned the premises, the plaintiff accepted rent for the premises from the second defendant, knowing that the second defendant was paying rent on his own behalf".

This paragraph discloses an arguable defence that Mr Best is now a tenant of the council but the council can find no records to support this allegation. A request for further and better particulars of the defence is needed to force Mr Best to make his allegations absolutely clear and to establish the possible merits of the defence. The defendant might be asked to state:

1. When it is alleged that the first defendant left the premises.

2. When it is alleged that the first defendant informed the plaintiff that he was leaving the premises and requested the said transfer, specifying whether the said communications were in writing or oral. If in writing, identify the document relied upon. If communicated orally, identify when, where and with whom the said conversation took place.

3. When it is alleged that the plaintiff first knew that it was receiving rent from the second defendant on the second defendant's own behalf, identifying each and every fact and matter relied upon in support of this contention.

If Mr Best answers these requests fully then the council will be in a much better position to check his allegations and find evidence which contradicts his case or perhaps realise that he has a good case which they ought to concede or settle. If he does not answer them, this may lead to him losing the case.

A request for further and better particulars must first be made by letter. If the party making the request is entitled to the further particulars they should be supplied. If they are not supplied, the party seeking the further and better particulars may go to court and seek an order requiring the defaulting party to answer the requests within a certain time.

Interrogatories

A request for further and better particulars targets certain facts relied upon by one party in the pleadings and asks for expansion. By contrast sometimes a party will want to know if a fact is agreed which is not in the pleadings, or at least what a party's position is on a particular fact. A common example arises where a paragraph alleging numerous facts in the particulars of claim is simply met by a flat denial of the whole paragraph in the defence. Each party is entitled to put questions to the other side. These questions are termed *interrogatories*.

Interrogatories must be answered on affidavit, and so are a useful method of obtaining admissions from the other side.

Example

Barcombe Housing Association let a flat to Mr Torwood. There have been numerous allegations of nuisance against Mr Torwood made by his neighbours, all of which are set out in paragraph 5 of the particulars of claim. Mr Torwood has filed a defence. The paragraph relating to paragraph 5 of the particulars of claim merely states "It is denied that the defendant has caused a nuisance or annoyance to his neighbours as alleged or at all". It is inconceivable to the association that none of the events pleaded took place, and they wish to know what the substance of the defence is. Interrogatories may be served to elicit exactly how Mr Torwood addresses each allegation (eg was he in the property at a particular time? Was there a party on a particular date at his house which finished at about 4 am the next day? and so on.)

Discovery

Discovery is the process by which each side discloses to the other all the documents which they have, or have had, in their possession, power or control which are (or may be) relevant to the action. Thus, both sides are compelled to disclose the documents upon which they intend to rely at trial with the result that neither side will be taken by surprise at the hearing by being confronted with a document which destroys or damages their contentions. It is not only documents favourable to a party's case which must be disclosed however. Most relevant documents must be provided on discovery (see further below for exceptions). As such, documents which tend to damage a party's own case must also be disclosed.

Filing

The process of discovery highlights the need for efficient management of housing files. Proper recording in files will ensure that discovery is a simple task. All the relevant documents should be on file and all that is required is that the file be copied for the defendant's benefit. Before this is done, privileged documents should be removed (see *Exceptions* below).The contents of the file will come under close scrutiny by the other side. Any notable gaps which are obvious from the file will be exploited by those advising the tenant who will be able to challenge the landlord's efficiency and methods. Similarly, documents of interest may arise but if they are not clearly dated their significance may be ambiguous. A memo or an attendance note lacking the name of the person who made it may cause considerable problems in finding the correct witness. Individual attendance notes or memoranda must be clearly written or typed, dated and signed.

It is accordingly important that files are kept thoroughly, up to date and in good condition. Files which are worn out or which do not have some form of clip for the documents inside them lead to crucial documents being lost and make the process of recording information far harder.

Discovery by lists

Discovery is commonly provided by lists of documents. Once each party is provided with the list, they are entitled at a later date to inspect the documents. All the relevant documents must be set out in the list, being identified by date, the maker of the document and the addressee. This information may all be self-evident from the documents themselves but housing officers should check the file for difficult documents, and, if possible, provide notes of clarification for the person preparing the list.

Exceptions

Not all documents have to be disclosed to the other side. There are a number of exceptions to the general principle that all relevant documents are subject to discovery. The most important exception in the context of possession actions is that documents prepared in contemplation of legal proceedings are not disclosed. Thus, letters to solicitors, or internal memoranda between a local authority's housing department and its legal department discussing the merits of bringing the possession proceedings are not shown to the other side.

Witness statements

In the vast majority of cases the parties will be required to provide witness statements well in advance of the hearing itself. The exchange of witness statements allows the parties to weigh up the merits of the case, thus inviting early settlement. The matters which remain in issue between the parties will also be more clearly defined. Crucially, the use of witness statements should prevent one party taking the other by surprise at the trial by bringing up matters which have not previously been considered. In general terms, the use of witness statements accordingly reduces the length of trials. In particular, it is now common practice for the judge to order that the witness statement will be allowed to stand as the evidence in chief, (ie the evidence that they would normally give under examination from their own lawyer, see chapter 6) of the witness who made the statement (CCR Order 20 rule 12A(7)(a). In High Court litigation this is now always the case.

The following points should be noted about the form

of witness statements and their use at court.

1. The statement must be dated and be signed by the maker of the statement and must include a statement by the witness that the contents are true to the best of his knowledge information and belief. It must also identify any documents which are referred to in the statement (CCR Order 20 rule 12A(1)(4)).

2. The statement should use numbered paragraphs for ease of reference.

3. The statement must include everything which is relevant, for a witness may only give evidence which is not included in the witness statement with the court's leave.

4. The use of witness statements in no way alters the normal rule of evidence that a witness may only give evidence of facts which are in his or her own knowledge and experience (ie *hearsay* evidence – see chapter 5 – must be excluded from the statement). Similarly a statement, subject to the use of the Civil Evidence Act 1968 procedure (see chapter 5) cannot be adduced without the witness being present.

Bearing this in mind, it is vitally important that the statement is well drafted and contains all the evidence that the witness can give and upon which the landlord wishes to rely. Given recent developments in the practice of the High Court, it is likely that the careful preparation of witness statements will be of increasing importance in the county court as well.

In practice, the actual statement prepared for use at court will be drafted by a lawyer but such a statement is usually based on a preliminary statement prepared by the housing officer. Accordingly, it is still necessary for the officer to bear in mind the points made above. It cannot be over-emphasised that the statement must be accurate in every respect. This may sound obvious, but lengthy statements must be thoroughly checked to ensure that all the information contained is correct for if it appears during cross-examination that there has been an inaccuracy, then the witness's credibility will be seriously undermined. If it appears to a housing officer at court that the statement includes a mistake, then such a mistake should be acknowledged and brought to the court's attention when the evidence is given in chief.

Unless orders

If one side fails to comply with any stage of the directions given, the other side may attempt to compel the dilatory party by applying to the court for an order threatening to strike out the plaintiff's claim or debar the defendant from further defending the action, **unless** the relevant party complies with the direction within a time specified in the order. In the event that a party fails to comply with the terms of the *unless order*, the innocent party may apply to the court for the order to be enforced.

The form on the order naturally depends on which procedural step has been breached.

Example
The plaintiff has failed to comply with a request for further and better particulars.
"Unless by 4 pm on 14th July 1995 the Plaintiff do

provide further and better particulars of the defence dated 3rd February 1995 the claim be struck be struck out".

The use of the *unless order* underlines the importance in complying with all the necessary procedural steps in time. Any housing officer when asked to comment on a pleading, answer interrogatories or provide a statement must be acutely aware of the importance of doing so as a matter or urgency. Any difficulties in complying with the order must be addressed at once. There is the possibility of extending the time for compliance with any of the time limits imposed by the County Court Rules, or by the court itself, under CCR Order 13 rule 4.

Typical directions

The directions which should be sought at the return date depend upon the nature of the case. The County Court Rules now provide set directions for certain types of case but these do not apply to possession actions. The following is typical of the sort of directions which might be made at a return date:

1. Defendant to file and serve a defence within 7 days of today.
2. Plaintiff to file and serve a reply within 14 days thereafter, if so advised.
3. Discovery by lists of documents within 28 days of today, inspection 7 days thereafter.
4. Witness statements to be exchanged between the parties within 56 days of today.
5. Matter to be set down on certificate of readiness of both parties with time estimate and list of witnesses.

Calculation of court time

When deciding whether the time-limit in the order has expired the County Court Rules (CCR Order 1 rule 9) set out the following principles for the computation of time:

1. Where an act is required to be done within a specified period **after** or **from** a specified date, the period begins **immediately after** the date specified.

2. Where an act is required to be done **within** or **not less than** a specified period before a specified date, the period ends **immediately before** that date.

3. If the period in question is three days or less, and would include a day on which the court office is closed, eg the weekend, that day is excluded.

4. Where the time limit fixed expires on a day on which the court office is closed, and for that reason the act cannot be done on that day, the act is in time if done on the next day on which the office is open.

CHAPTER 5

EVIDENCE

Burden of proof / Types of evidence / ***Hearsay / Informal admission / Public documents / Evidence under Civil Evidence Act / Affidavit evidence / Expert evidence***

As has been emphasised, the main role of housing managers or officers in presenting contested possession proceedings is to ensure that all the evidence which is available has been brought to the attention of the lawyers conducting the case. The court may only make a decision on the evidence before it which it is entitled to look at. This chapter therefore examines the rules relating to evidence.

Burden of proof

Housing managers must consider at an early stage whether or not there is sufficient evidence to prove each element of the case. In civil litigation, it is for the party who is asserting a fact to prove it. Accordingly, in possession actions it is normally the landlord as plaintiff, who bears the burden of proof. If the landlord cannot provide evidence about a particular element which must be proved, the case will be lost. At the return date hearing, even if the defendant does not attend, it is still possible for the landlord to be unsuccessful because the burden of proof is on the landlord. The burden will not be on the landlord where it is for the defendant to prove a positive case. Accordingly, in a case brought against a trespasser, once the landlord has proven title to the property it is then for the defendant to prove that he or she has obtained some form of interest.

In civil cases, the standard of proof is *on the balance of probabilities*, ie the person proving a fact must show that it was more probable than not that what is alleged took place. In a case where the judge finds both versions equally likely, the party upon whom the burden of proof lies will lose. If the conduct alleged is of a criminal character, eg fraud, the standard of proof technically remains the same but the judge will look for a slightly higher level of proof while not requiring proof *beyond reasonable doubt*. This may be relevant in cases brought under Ground 5 of Schedule 2 to the Housing Act 1985 (tenancy obtained by deception).

Types of evidence

Evidence can come in many forms – oral testimony, written statement, documents and so on. In relation to witnesses the general rule is that their evidence must be given orally (see further below as to exceptions to this). It is thus important that at the trial, all witnesses are in court to give their evidence.

Case report

At the trial of an action for possession on the basis of rent arrears, the London Borough of Lambeth alleged arrears of £4,399. The only evidence in court was a computer print-out of the rent account history. No application had been made to have this admitted without any oral evidence (under the Civil Evidence Act 1968, see below) nor was any witness available in court to prove or explain the account. The tenant objected to the admission of the print-out. The council did not apply to adjourn and the claim was dismissed with the consequence that the amount due is now irrecoverable.

Lambeth LBC v White 1995 June *Legal Action*, p19.

The law of evidence can be highly technical and complex but an understanding of certain basic principles is essential if housing managers and officers are to be able to prepare cases properly. Problems may arise if at a late stage in the preparation of a case it becomes apparent that, because of the rules of evidence, matters which might have been put to the court by the landlord are ruled as inadmissible. The main rule that it is necessary to be aware of is that of *hearsay*.

Hearsay

The primary rule is that witnesses may only give evidence about what they themselves have either heard or seen. If the fact which witnesses want to talk about is not in their experience then it cannot be given in evidence. Evidence which is derived from other sources – *second hand* – is not admissible in court and cannot be relied upon by the party adducing it; this is subject to certain exceptions which are considered later. Such evidence is referred to as hearsay evidence.

It is accordingly important that, in preparing a case, the housing officer look carefully at whether or not it is information which he or she can give evidence of first hand. All too often there may be a useful note on file which an officer might wish to rely on but which was recorded by someone else. This is a particular problem often encountered by social landlords, as relevant information may have accrued over a number of years and numerous officers (some of whom may have left) may have dealt with one property.

A clear demonstration of the importance of the hearsay rule arises in cases involving harassment. The single major problem for landlords in trying to deal with incidents of racial harassment arises from the identification of the perpetrators of the acts. The complaint is often that most people know who committed the act but no-one saw it, or no-one who saw it is prepared to go to court to give evidence. Suspicion and rumour will not suffice: they amount to hearsay.

The definition of hearsay is "an out of court statement tendered for the truth of its contents". Housing officers who find that reference is being made to something which was told to them should be alert to the fact that they might be straying into hearsay evidence. However, such evidence is only inadmissible in so far as the landlord wishes to adduce it for the facts contained.

Example

Marmsbury Borough Council are bringing possession proceedings against Mr Jameson for nuisance and annoyance to neighbours. The housing officer (Ms Khan) conducting the case may give evidence of the complaints made to her by Mr Jameson's neighbours, even though they are out-of-court statements. However, in saying that complaints were made to her and the nature of the conduct complained of, she is not doing so to prove that there was a nuisance but only to explain her own subsequent involvement and the reason why she then visited Mr Jameson and discussed matters with him. Only the neighbours can give evidence that there was a nuisance, because only they have first hand knowledge that a nuisance occurred.

Informal admission

The main exception to the hearsay rule is any statement made by a party to the proceedings. This is known as an *informal admission* (informal as opposed to a formal admission made in the pleadings). Thus, housing managers or officers may give evidence of the contents of a conversation with a defendant. A housing officer may, for example, be able to give evidence concerning a conversation with an unlawful occupier which contradicts the case which the unlawful occupier is relying on before the court.

Public documents

Public documents which are kept by officials who are under a duty to ensure the truth of their contents comprise another important exception to the hearsay rule. Thus, a death certificate is admissible evidence to show that a tenant has deceased. A certificate of conviction from the clerk of a court may be produced to show that a tenant committed a particular offence in a case based on nuisance to neighbours.

Evidence under Civil Evidence Act

There are occasions when it is simply not possible for the person who has first hand knowledge of the evidence to be at court to give oral evidence. The Civil Evidence Act 1968 provides that, in certain limited circumstances, hearsay evidence may be given to the court. This allows a party to produce documents, even full statements, without the maker of the document giving evidence, or for a witness to give evidence of what he or she was told by someone who will not be attending the court.

A party who intends to rely on hearsay evidence at the trial must serve a notice not less than 14 days before the hearing. This does not apply if a defence has not been filed. If the statement is contained in a document, a copy must be attached to the notice, which must specify:

1. the time, place and circumstances at or in which the statement was made;

2. the name of the maker of the statement and to whom the statement was made (unless this information is patently obvious from the statement itself).

If the party giving notice alleges that the maker of the statement cannot be called as a witness, the notice must include a statement setting out the reason why. The five permissible reasons are that the witness:

1. is dead; or

2. is beyond the seas; or

3. is unfit, by reason of his or her bodily or mental condition, to attend as a witness; or

4. cannot with reasonable diligence be identified or found; or

5. cannot reasonably be expected (having regard to the time which has elapsed since he was connected or concerned as aforesaid and to all the circumstances) to have any recollection of matters relevant to the accuracy or otherwise of the statement.

It is to be noted that these are the only reasons. The fact that an officer is no longer in the landlord's employment is not sufficient.

The party receiving the notice may, within seven days after service of the notice, serve and file at court a counter-notice requiring the person stated to be the maker of the statement in the notice to be called as a witness at court. If the party serving the counter-notice believes that the reason stated in the notice for the witness being unable to attend court does not apply, then the counter-notice must state this.

Where a counter-notice is served, the party seeking to rely on the hearsay evidence will not in general be allowed to adduce the evidence unless one of the specified reasons applies. The court does, however, have a discretion to allow the hearsay evidence to be adduced in any event and even has a further discretion to dispense with the notice procedure altogether. Obviously, the circumstances in which the discretion is exercised will be limited and it is always best to ensure that the notice is served if possible, for otherwise the court may consider that a tactical advantage is being sought by the party attempting to adduce the hearsay evidence.

Affidavit evidence

Whilst the primary rule is that evidence is given orally to the court, there are times when affidavit evidence may be used. Its chief use in possession proceedings is at the return date, where it may save the attendance of a housing manager or officer at court. An obvious example arises where the manager or officer who has conduct of the case did not serve the notice seeking possession. It would be a waste of time for the person who served the notice to attend court when a simple affidavit stating how the notice was served and exhibiting the notice to the affidavit would suffice.

There are situations relating to procedural matters in which a housing officer will need to file affidavit evidence rather than give oral evidence. This will be required when answering interrogatories or explaining to the court the absence of a lost document which should be disclosed, or in answering a defendant's affidavit in support of an application to set aside an order for possession.

Expert evidence

Witnesses give evidence of the facts they perceived; they do not give opinions. Where, however, a matter before the court calls for expertise in a particular field, a suitably qualified person may be called to give evidence including his or her opinion.

The following are examples of experts who may sometimes be useful.

Environmental health officers

They are useful in cases involving tenants who are a nuisance to neighbours or who have allowed the condition of the premises to deteriorate, for they are able to give evidence on the risks caused to the community at large by anti-social behaviour. Issues they address include:

- the harbouring of rubbish in dwellings creating the risk of infestations of mice, cockroaches and other vermin.
- keeping pets in poor conditions, keeping unsuitable

pets and the risks of illness caused by allowing dogs to foul common parts.

- noise levels, and whether or not a statutory nuisance has been created. (See A. Kilpatrick *Repairs and Maintenance*, Arden's Housing Library vol.5, 1996).

Handwriting experts

Sometimes much will turn on whether or not a document is authentic. If provided with a suitable sample, a handwriting expert may be able to identify whether or not the document was written by a particular person.

Surveyors

The tenant may seek to argue that the damage has been caused by disrepair to the premises for which the landlord is responsible. Surveyors can give their opinion on the cause of the damage to the property. (See generally, P. Reddin *Dealing with Housing Disrepair: a guide to inspection and diagnosis* Arden's Housing Library, vol.6, 1996).

They will be needed in a rent arrears case where there is a disrepair counterclaim. Expert evidence is also required in claims where the landlord intends to do works to the property, and requires vacant possession (Ground 10 of Schedule 2 to the Housing Act 1985).

Medical evidence

Sometimes the evidence of doctors may be required to comment on the health of the tenant and their housing needs, or those of the tenant's family. This may be relevant to the issue of the suitability of alternative accommodation in cases where this must be provided.

Medical opinion may be needed to assess whether someone would be better re-housed in sheltered accommodation in the type of case where the ground for possession is nuisance to neighbours, or deterioration to the premises.

CHAPTER 6

THE TRIAL

Settlement / Judges / Giving evidence / ***The oath*** **/ The opening / Landlord's case /** ***Evidence-in-chief*** **/** ***Cross-examination*** **/** ***Re-examination*** **/ Defence case / Closing speeches**

The aim of this chapter is to set out how a full trial is conducted. It must be emphasised that housing managers and officers are more than just witnesses. They are also the representatives of the landlord, having initiated the proceedings. Accordingly, they will need to be present throughout the trial, both to comment on any matters which may arise during the defendant's evidence and provide any additional information which may be required.

In outline the process is as follows:
1. The landlord's lawyer opens the case.
2. The landlord's evidence is presented.
Each witness will be sworn in, give his or her evidence in chief, and then be cross-examined. Witnesses

may then be re-examined by their own lawyers.

3. The same process occurs with the defendant's witnesses.

4. Each side, with the defendant going before the plaintiff, will make closing speeches.

Settlement

Possession actions rarely, by their very nature, settle, in part because it is not possible to contract out of the security of tenure provisions provided by the Housing Acts, and therefore a court order is required (see chapter 10, on the making of consent orders) but mainly because it will usually be so difficult for the tenant to find somewhere else to live. In certain cases, however, it will be necessary for housing managers to ensure that they have authority to reach a settlement in matters. This may be the case in a rent arrears case where there is a disrepair counterclaim. Such actions often result in a settlement, and housing managers and officers must ensure that they have been authorised to waive arrears of rent to a certain level or indeed pay the defendant damages in addition.

Judges

Possession proceedings are before a judge or a district judge. All county court judges (also referred to as *circuit judges*) should be addressed as "Your Honour"; district judges should be addressed as "Sir" or "Madam".

Giving evidence

When giving evidence certain basic points must be remembered. The questions will come from the legal representatives in front of the housing manager or officer, but answers should be directed to the judge, who will be sitting to the side of the witness box. Although proceedings may well be recorded on tape, the judge will always be taking a full handwritten note of the evidence given. Evidence must be given slowly and clearly. It is always advisable to watch the judge's hand to see if he or she is still writing before continuing with a new sentence.

The Oath

All evidence is given *on oath*, ie before the witness gives evidence it is necessary to swear by the book appropriate to the witness's religion that the evidence will be the truth. Witnesses who do not have a religion may simply *affirm*, ie promise solemnly to tell the truth.

The opening

The landlord's legal representative introduces the case, taking the judge through the pleadings and identifying the issues which are to be decided. The judge should be taken through all the documents which will be referred to during the course of the evidence, which should be in a paginated bundle. A copy of the bundle is made available to the witnesses when they give their evidence.

Landlord's case

In civil trials the plaintiff gives evidence first, and is then followed by the defendant's case.

Evidence-in-chief

Each witness is called in turn and gives his or her evidence. This is referred to as *evidence in chief*. How evidence in chief is conducted will depend upon whether or not the parties, and the judge, wish the witness statements (see chapter 4) to stand as the witnesses' evidence in chief. After being sworn in (see above), the housing manager or officer will be asked to give his or her full name, occupation and address (a work address only need be given).

If it is indicated that the statements are to be used as the evidence in chief, then this part of the trial is very simple. The housing officer will be directed to his or her statement in the witness bundle, and will be asked to confirm the signature at the bottom and to confirm that the contents of the statement are true. At this point, if there are any mistakes in the statement they should be brought to the court's attention.

If the statements are not to stand as evidence in chief, then evidence in chief is a much more lengthy process. The legal representative asks the housing officer questions designed to bring out all the evidence contained in the statement but it is not permissible to refer to the statement. Whilst the questions asked are designed to provoke answers which cover all the information, the housing officer should bear in mind the information which needs to be given in evidence. In evidence in chief a legal representative is not allowed to ask *leading questions*, ie questions which themselves suggest the answer to the defendant.

Cross-examination

Cross-examination is the opportunity for the defendant's legal representative to question the landlord's witnesses. Wherever there is a factual dispute between the parties, the legal representative will put the defendant's version of events to the housing officer. Most importantly, the defendant's representative will seek to undermine the reliability of the housing officer's evidence. In many cases, this will consist of identifying gaps in the housing file, by pointing out notes of meetings one would expect to find or indicating that records of conversations with the defendant are incomplete. The implication is, of course, that if the housing file can be shown not to contain the whole story, then the defendant's version of events which may not be consistent with the records on the housing file becomes more credible. Of course, no housing file can be perfect but the importance of keeping full and proper records is highlighted.

In cross-examination leading questions are allowed. Indeed, they are at the heart of the skill of good cross-examination. Ideally, the witness is led down a path of simple questions to which the answer is yes or no, until the witness adopts a position which is no longer consistent with the statement given in examination in chief. In answering such questions the housing officer should be wary of agreeing too readily with the suggestions which are put: if a question cannot be answered with a simple yes or no, then a fuller explanation should be provided. Similarly, if a housing officer is asked about an area of information of which he or she has no knowledge this must be admitted. Sometimes it will be clear that another witness will be able to deal with such matters and it will be possible to indicate that the question should be addressed to that witness. On the other hand, the housing officer should not be unnecessarily antagonistic towards the defendant's legal representative.

Where there is more than one defendant, the first defendant's representative will cross-examine first. In reality, it is unusual for possession actions to involve multiple parties who require separate representation. Where the defendants are joint tenants they are unlikely to have a conflicting interest and will normally be represented by the same person.

Re-examination

After cross-examination, the landlord's representative has the opportunity of asking questions on matters which arose from evidence given under cross-examination. This is an opportunity to regain any ground which may have been lost. Finally, the judge may ask some questions. After giving evidence it is possible for the housing officer formally to be released from having to remain at the trial. Commonly, however, even though the officer may be released it will be necessary for the officer to remain to give instructions about points raised during the defendant's evidence.

Defence case

The defendant presents his or her case in exactly the same way. Each witness gives evidence in the same way as the landlord's witnesses. Housing officers should be ready to indicate to the barrister or solicitor any points which occur to them which might be put in cross-examination.

Closing speeches

The legal representatives then summarise the evidence which has been before the court, indicating how the evidence best supports their version of events, and address the judge on the relevant law. The defendant's speech comes before the plaintiff's. Subsequently, the judge will deliver judgment or may, if the matter is complicated or time is short, indicate that judgment is reserved to another day. After judgment, the terms of the order to be made – including the question of costs – will be addressed by the representatives of each party, and the judge will make an order.

PART II

POSSESSION PROCEDURE: TYPES OF CASES

CHAPTER 7

RENT ARREARS CASES

Statutory grounds / Required evidence / *Evidence of arrears* / **Options for orders** / *Arrears cleared / Arrears substantially cleared and agreement about remainder / Arrears at significant level / Very significant arrears* / **Defences** / *Disrepair / Housing benefit / Landlord and Tenant Act 1987*

Rent arrears cases are now commonly presented by housing managers or officers without the aid of legal representation. The majority of what follows is equally applicable to managers or officers who attend as witnesses or as representatives of the landlord.

Statutory grounds

The statutory grounds for rent arrears are ground 1 of schedule 2 to the Housing Act 1985 for secure tenancies, and Grounds 8, 10 and 11 of Schedule 2 to the Housing Act 1988 for assured tenancies. In order to succeed in establishing that Ground 1 has been made out, the landlord has to prove that rent lawfully due has not been paid. The court will then proceed to consider whether or not it is reasonable in all the circumstances to make an order for possession.

Landlords of assured tenancies are in a stronger position in that Ground 8 is a mandatory ground for possession, ie once the ground is established the court must make an order for possession and does not consider the question of reasonableness. Ground 8 is available to the landlord if – both at the date of service of the notice seeking possession and at the date of the hearing of the action – an amount of rent, calculated as set out below, is outstanding:

- if rent is payable fortnightly – at least 13 weeks' rent;
- if rent is payable monthly – at least three months' rent;
- if rent is payable quarterly – at least one quarter's rent is more than three months in arrears;
- if rent is payable yearly – at least three months' rent is more than three months in arrears.

A landlord intending to rely upon Ground 8 must include the ground in the notice seeking possession (the court may not exercise its discretion to dispense with the notice if ground 8 is be relied upon).

An assured landlord who is not entitled to rely upon Ground 8 must base its case upon Grounds 10 and/or 11, which are often both applicable. Ground 10 applies where some rent lawfully due from the tenant:

(a) is unpaid on the date on which the proceeding for possession are begun; and

(b) is unpaid at the date of service of the notice seeking possession.

Ground 11 is available to the landlord whether or not any rent is in arrears on the date possession proceedings are begun. The landlord must prove that the tenant has persistently delayed in paying rent which has become lawfully due. This ground provides a useful remedy to a landlord who is faced by a tenant who has a bad record of payment but who pays off the arrears, or the majority of them, once possession proceedings are commenced.

Required evidence

Obviously, the housing officer needs to attend with the housing file and in particular have the following documents:

1. the tenancy agreement. This is evidence of the landlord's title, but may also be needed to show the definition of rent in the agreement, the time when rent was to be paid or even to show that the tenant had an address at which to serve the landlord with proceedings (see section 48 of the Landlord and Tenant Act 1987, see further below).

2. the notice seeking possession and proof of service.

3. print-outs of the rent account showing the position as of the date of the hearing (a copy each for the officer, the judge and the tenant).

4. any agreement made with the tenant regarding payment of arrears.

5. any information regarding housing benefit (if applicable) and information as to the tenant's current employment status.

Evidence of arrears

When presenting evidence about the arrears, it is always vital to make clear to the court the difference between the *contractual rent*, and the rent which the tenant is actually liable to pay (often referred to as the *rebated rent*).

Some computerised rent accounts also distinguish between the *gross rent*, and the *net rent*. The net rent is the charge made for the use of the dwelling. However, the tenancy agreement may include other charges which are within the definition of rent in the tenancy agreement. Common examples are charges for heating, or the employment of a caretaker. The actual rent charged is commonly referred to as the gross rent.

Those advising tenants have often sought to distinguish the net rent and the gross rent to show that the ground for possession has not been made out or that the notice seeking possession is defective. Much will turn on the facts of each case and what charges are included in the rent as defined in the tenancy agreement. It is thought, however, that as long as the definition of rent in the tenancy agreement is sufficiently precise, this argument should not succeed. Additionally, with regard to secure tenancies, Ground 1 of Schedule 2 to the Housing Act 1985 is made out if any obligation of the tenancy is broken, whether it is the covenant to pay rent or any other charge under the agreement.

Options for orders

Most rent arrears claims may be dealt with swiftly by the court. Various options are available to the landlord and the court depending upon the efforts made by the tenant prior to the hearing. It is impossible to cover all of the permutations which may arise; the following is intended as a guide to the range of orders which may be made.

Arrears cleared

For example – where the tenant has paid off all, or virtually all, of the rent arrears and it is clear to the landlord that there is unlikely to be further default. In these circumstances clearly the landlord will not succeed in obtaining a possession order. The landlord may wish to withdraw the proceedings or, alternatively, to ask that the matter be adjourned with liberty to restore. The latter course has the advantage of ensuring that if the tenant subsequently lapses into rent arrears again, the landlord is able to take swift action without having to waste time and money in re-commencing proceedings. If, however, the landlord is a local authority, and it is obvious that the arrears have accrued because of delays in the award of housing benefit, the proceedings should probably be withdrawn.

Arrears substantially cleared and agreement about remainder

For example – the tenant has not paid off all the arrears, but has reduced them to a reasonable level and has reached a satisfactory agreement regarding the payment of arrears plus current rent. The arrears are of a level which would not justify the court making an order for possession.

The court has the power to adjourn possession actions on such terms as it considers to be fit (section

85(1) of the Housing Act 1985, or section 9(1) of the Housing Act 1988). The court should be provided with the terms of any agreement and invited to adjourn the action on the terms of that agreement. When such an agreement has been reached, tenants may be told that there is no need for them to attend the hearing.

The order is commonly in the following form: "The matter be adjourned on terms that the Defendant pay the current rent of £x per week plus £y per week off the arrears".

If the tenant subsequently breaches the terms of the agreement the landlord will be able to return to court and prove its case. (See also subsequent conduct by parties in chapter 11 below).

Arrears at significant level

For example – the arrears as at the date of the hearing are sufficient to warrant an order for possession being made by the court, but not so high as to warrant an *outright order* for possession. The overwhelming majority of possession cases based upon rent arrears are concluded by some form of *suspended order*. (Indeed, action ought to be taken by housing officers before arrears rise to the level which would justify an outright rather than a suspended order).

Difficulties may be encountered in persuading the court that it is justified in making an order for possession at all. Some judges, if the arrears are not in their view significant enough to warrant an order, suggest an adjournment on terms or decide that only a money judgment should be made. The issue is one of reasonableness and the level of the arrears is an important consideration. The emphasis by the landlord must be on the need to have a real threat over the tenant which can only be provided by the granting of a suspended order (see further chapter 10, below). To justify this, it will be necessary to provide details of the past record of payment, and earlier failures to make agreements with the landlord about the payment of arrears or to keep to agreements made.

Very significant arrears

For example – the level of arrears is such that the landlord wishes to obtain an outright order. Social landlords may often find it difficult to obtain an outright order. Whilst most judges will warn tenants severely about the level of arrears which have accrued, sometimes the very level of the arrears backfires on the landlord. Judges often express the view that a responsible landlord should not have allowed the arrears to accrue to such a high level.

It may well not be in the landlord's interests to obtain an outright order. If a suspended order is made, even though the rent arrears may take years to be paid off, there is always the prospect that the landlord will recoup its money. When an outright order is made the landlord will also be granted a money judgment for the arrears, but that may prove very difficult to enforce against someone who will prove difficult to trace and who may have no incentive to pay off any of the judgment.

In all rent arrears cases the judge will bear in mind that the tenant will be losing his or her home. If a possession order is made on the basis of rent arrears, the tenant may well subsequently not be owed a duty by the local authority to be provided with accommodation, as he or she may well be deemed to be intentionally homeless (depending on how the arrears arose). Individuals who grant tenancies rely on the rent for income. In general terms – and individual judges vary in their views – the courts expect social landlords to have a much higher degree of tolerance regarding arrears. The courts are acutely aware of the problem of homelessness in the country today.

This does not mean that it is impossible to seek an outright order. The landlord will need to emphasise the level of arrears, but that alone is not conclusive. Of particular significance is the tenant's payment record. Housing managers need to be in the position where they can summarise when the last payment was made by the tenant, and be able to demonstrate how little over a period of months the tenant has paid.

Local authority landlords when dealing with the issue of reasonableness may refer to the effect of the Local Government and Housing Act 1989, under which local authorities are now required to balance their housing revenue accounts. The failure of one tenant to pay the rent necessarily leads to a rent increase for other, reliable tenants.

Defences

The following are the three defences which may be raised.

Disrepair

Some tenants withhold payment of rent out of frustration with landlords who fail to carry out their obligations under the repairing covenants. A tenant who is in rent arrears may make a counterclaim for damages which may then be set off against any rent arrears recovered. A tenant may seek to raise this argument even as late as the return date itself, and will usually be granted an adjournment to file a properly pleaded defence and counterclaim. In these circumstances a social landlord should seek to ensure that an *unless order* (see chapter 4) is made. Such actions subsequently turn on the merits of the claim for damages for disrepair (for the law relating to disrepair see A. Kilpatrick *Repairs and Maintenance*, Arden's Housing Library vol.5, 1996).

A difficult situation arises if the landlord of an assured tenancy is able to show that Ground 8 is made out at the return date, but the tenant asserts that there is a claim for damages for disrepair. Ground 8 is a mandatory ground for possession; and it might be argued that, if it can be proved to the court that the rent is lawfully due then an order for possession should be made, even though the tenant may have a claim for damages (which can be pursued separately). There is no definitive ruling on this point, but it is thought that a court would probably adjourn the possession action pending the result of the counterclaim, unless it was obvious that the counterclaim could not possibly reduce the arrears to a level below that required for ground 8 to apply. (This view is based on observations made by the Court of Appeal in *Mountain v Hastings* (1993) 25 HLR 427).

Housing benefit

Tenants on low income, or on income support, may be entitled to housing benefit. If the landlord is a local housing authority the benefit takes the form of a rent rebate. Otherwise, the benefit will normally be paid to the tenant by the housing benefit department, although in certain circumstances it may be paid directly.

Sometimes there is a considerable delay in the processing of an application for housing benefit. This does not, of course, alter the fact that the tenant remains contractually liable to pay the full rent and it is no defence to the possession claim that the housing benefit has not been paid. Many judges will, however, look sympathetically on tenants whose arrears are claimed to be due to delays in housing benefit and will often adjourn the case while the position is sorted out. This is particularly true where the landlord is the local authority who administers the housing benefit.

It is important therefore to determine whether the delay has been caused by the housing benefit section or by the tenant's failure to complete the application form properly or provide requested documents. Where it is known that housing benefit may be an issue, full details should be sought from the housing benefit section about the correct level of payment and the exact position of the claim. Once a query has been made, the judge will undoubtedly ask a local authority housing officer what exactly the position is in regard to housing benefit. It is always good practice to come prepared for the question.

In exceptional cases the local authority has the discretion to backdate benefit payments for up to 12 months. It may agree to do so if the tenant has failed to make an application due to illness, or because of complete ignorance of the availability of benefit. If backdating is being considered then the court may be unwilling to make a possession order until a determination has been reached. Often in such a case, the court will adjourn the matter pending the outcome of the decision on backdating.

Landlord and Tenant Act 1987

Section 48 of the Landlord and Tenant Act 1987 places a specific requirement on landlords to supply tenants with a notice of an address in England or Wales at which notices (including of legal proceedings) may be served on them. Under section 48(2) where the landlord has failed to comply with this requirement any rent due from the tenant is to be treated for all purposes as not being due.

In most cases the requirement will be complied with by the inclusion of the landlord's name and address in the tenancy agreement (see *Rogan v Woodfield Building Services* (1994) 27 HLR 78, CA). It is important to ensure therefore that proof of the service of the address either in the tenancy agreement or by some other means is available so that the tenant cannot raise a defence under this section. Failure to serve the required notice does not destroy the right to recover the rent, but merely postpones it until a notice has been served: *Dallhold Estates (UK) Pty. Inc. v Lindsey Trading Properties Inc.* [1994] 1 EGLR 93 CA.

CHAPTER 8

OTHER TYPES OF POSSESSION ACTION

Unauthorised occupiers / *Required evidence* / *Defences which may be raised* / *Money judgment* / *Return date* / **Nuisance and annoyance** / *Witness statement* / *Return date* / *Undertakings*

In this chapter two further types of possession action are discussed:

- those against unauthorised occupiers
- those on the basis of nuisance and annoyance.

Unauthorised occupiers

An *unauthorised occupier* is a person who resides in premises, but who has no contractual right or permission from the owner so to do. Although it is a phrase commonly used by those in housing management, it is not a legal term. Such a person is in law referred to as a *trespasser*. Unauthorised occupier is a term generally used in housing management to apply to occupiers who entered the premises with the consent of the tenant, but who have ceased to have a right to remain in the property because the tenant's interest has been determined.

There are numerous ways in which housing managers may find out that a property is being occupied by someone other than the tenant, whilst the tenant has gone away. If the tenant has left, arrears of rent may accrue and a routine visit to discuss the arrears position may lead to the discovery that the tenant has abandoned the property. Sometimes the tenant writes notifying the landlord that he or she will be leaving to live elsewhere. This is often accompanied by a request to transfer the tenancy to a person residing with the tenant. That person may be entitled to an assignment of the tenancy (see C. Hunter *Tenants' Rights*, Arden's Housing Library vol.2, 1995). If not, once the tenant's interest has been properly determined the persons who remain in occupation will be trespassers who have no right to remain in the property.

Required evidence

Possession proceedings brought against unlawful occupiers require little to be established by the landlord. Once it can be shown that the contractual tenant has ceased to live in the property, the contractual tenancy ceases to be secure and may therefore be determined by notice to quit. If the contractual tenancy is properly determined, then the interest of any person residing with the tenant is also determined.

Rights of spouses

One significant exception to this general statement arises in the case of matrimonial homes. If a sole tenant abandons a property leaving his or her spouse in occupation, the spouse is able to keep the tenancy alive by continuing to make payments (see section 1(5) of the Matrimonial Homes Act 1983).

Proof in court

Apart from the above exception, it is only necessary to for the landlord to prove two matters to the court to be entitled to a possession order:

1. the contractual tenant no longer occupies the property as the only or principal home; and

2. a notice to quit in the prescribed form has been served on the tenant.

Defences

Complications often arise in possession actions of this type. In broad terms, the defences used may be divided into two types:

1. the occupier asserts that the tenant has not left the property permanently, and so has not lost security of tenure;

2. the occupier asserts that by its conduct the landlord has granted a tenancy to the occupier.

Temporarily absent tenant

It is essential to the concept of a tenancy that the tenant may invite on to the property whomsoever he or she wishes (provided, of course, that in so doing the property does not become statutorily overcrowded and there is no nuisance to neighbours). As well as the tenant's immediate family, there may be temporary visitors or even lodgers. Section 93(1) of the Housing Act 1985 makes it a term of any secure tenancy that the tenant may allow persons to reside as lodgers in the dwelling-house.

In addition, a lodger may act as a caretaker for a tenant, keeping the tenant's security of tenure alive whilst the tenant is temporarily away. As long as the tenant genuinely intends to return, the lodger's presence will ensure that the tenancy remains secure or assured.

Housing managers will need to gather evidence to check the explanation provided by an occupier claiming to be keeping alive the tenancy. An absent tenant may only continue to be secure, or assured, if (see further A. Dymond *Security of Tenure*, ch 4, Arden's Housing Library vol.1, 1995):

1. the tenant genuinely intends to return to the property; and

2. there is evidence of continued occupation.

The occupier should be asked to explain:

- when he or she first went into occupation of the property;
- the terms of the agreement between the tenant and the occupier, including any financial arrangements, to establish whether the occupier resided with the tenant at some point or is a subtenant;
- who else is residing in the property;
- the whereabouts of the tenant providing a telephone number and address if possible;
- the reason for the tenant's absence, and when the tenant will be returning.

All this evidence must be clearly recorded. Most social landlords provide set forms for officers to use for unlawful occupier cases. As a result of the interview the housing officer may realise that action must be taken immediately, because the tenant has lost security.

Difficulties may arise where the occupier claims that the tenant will be returning. The occupier's story must be checked, and it will be necessary to try to trace the tenant. Neighbours may be able to provide helpful evidence as to where the tenant might be.

Creation of new tenancy

Occupiers may assert that the landlord has known for some time about their occupation, and state that they have been paying the rent. The argument in such a case is that where someone has exclusive possession of a property and is making payments referable to a period, a tenancy has been created. It is not enough however for the occupier to demonstrate that some payments have been made into the rent account. The reason for this is obvious. There is no requirement that a payment of rent be made by the tenant in person. It would be absurd if this were the case. Consider the case of older or disabled tenants who get friends or relatives to make the payments on their behalf.

Another fact often relied upon by occupiers is that they have called the landlord's maintenance department, and have had repairs done to the property at their request. Again this alone does not demonstrate that a tenancy has been created with the occupier. There is no reason why a lodger or relative should not report disrepair to the landlord.

In order to show that a new tenancy has been created it will be necessary for the occupier to establish both that the old tenancy has been determined, and that he or she has been granted a new tenancy. The occupier will need to prove two factors to the court, namely that:

1. the landlord had notice of the fact that the tenant had left the property, and **left permanently**;

2. after the landlord knew that the tenant had left permanently, the landlord, without protest, accepted rent from the occupier in the knowledge that the rent was tendered on the occupier's **own behalf** (*see Tower Hamlets LBC v Ayinde* (1994) 26 HLR 23 CA).

Unless there is clear evidence of this on file (which will be unlikely), the difficulty for the housing officer is showing that the occupier's assertions are incorrect if not a complete fabrication. The burden, however, will be on the tenant to show that what is alleged is true, but the landlord cannot leave the occupier's contentions unaddressed.

Often difficulties arise because the occupier relies on a conversation with a housing officer which took place some time ago. If the same officer is still in charge of the property then there should be no difficulty. He or she can give evidence to the effect that such a conversation did or did not take place and that it could not have taken place with anyone else. However, personnel changes can create problems, particularly for local authority landlords, who may have had to address numerous organisational changes. It is important for records to be kept of the whereabouts of former employees, should the evidence subsequently become required.

The occupier should be pressed to provide the name of the officer concerned, although failure to provide a name will not necessarily be taken by the court to indicate fabrication by the occupier. If a name cannot be supplied then a description should be ascertained. It may be possible for someone to confirm that no-one matching the tenant's description of the officer was working in relation to the particular property at the time of the alleged conversation.

Cases of this type emphasise the need to keep the records on the housing file properly. The landlord's case is usually that it was never aware that the original tenant had left the property, for if such knowledge had come to the attention of the housing officer at the time then action would have been taken and the information would have been kept on file. The fact that there is no record on file shows that the occupier's version of events is incorrect. Those acting for the occupier will be able severely to undermine this argument if it can be shown that other records are not on file which should be.

Cases of this type also highlight the importance of keeping a good record of the initial interview with the unlawful occupier, as it may be possible to show inconsistencies between what was initially said by the occupier and the case relied upon at court.

Local authority housing officers should be aware of using information from other departments. Indeed, the defendant will normally wish to obtain discovery of documents from such departments to show that they were aware of his or her presence in the property. Such evidence may support the local authority's case. By way of example, a lodger may have applied for housing through the waiting list whilst living at the property. If that application has not been withdrawn, it is arguably inconsistent with the contention that the authority knew that the defendant was paying rent on his or her own behalf rather than that of the contractual tenant. Investigations with the housing benefit department may also provide information inconsistent with the defendant's assertions.

Money judgment

In addition to a possession order, the landlord will normally be seeking some form of money judgment in a case of this type. Indeed, officers often first discover that a tenant has left because they are investigating rent arrears.

It is crucial to distinguish between *rent arrears* and *damages for use and occupation*. When an officer is satisfied that the tenant is no longer occupying the premises – and it is being occupied by a trespasser – the officer must serve a notice to quit determining the contractual tenancy and write to the occupier giving notification that the contractual tenancy has been determined, and that – unless the occupier leaves the property – possession proceedings will be commenced. In addition, the rent account should be stopped and the letter to the occupier must state that any money received by the landlord from the occupier will be accepted on account out of the damages for use and occupation which will be sought against the occupier.

In preparing for trial, the housing officer should firstly ascertain the amount of arrears at the time of the expiry of the notice to quit. Any such sum may be claimed against the tenant and – although it is not strictly necessary to join the tenant as party to the proceedings for the purpose of gaining a possession order – if it is intended to seek a judgment for arrears of rent against the tenant then that person must be joined as a defendant.

After the expiry of the notice to quit, the occupier becomes a trespasser. The landlord is entitled to obtain an order for damages for use and occupation of the property from the occupier from that date. The amount of the damages to be claimed is calculated by reference to the amount of the rent payable by the tenant prior to the expiry of the notice to quit. It may take some time before the case comes to trial and during this period the landlord would have increased the contractual rent if there had been a tenant in the property. If this is so, the landlord is entitled to claim damages for use and occupation at the rate at which the new rent would have been from the time when the rent would have been increased.

A significant time may elapse before the case is finally determined. Whatever the result of the case the occupier will be liable to pay for the use of the dwelling (whether by way of damages for use and occupation or rent). The landlord may apply for an order that the defendant make payments pending the outcome of the action under CCR Order 13, rule 12.

Example

Mr and Mrs Miller were the tenants of a council flat let to them by Bradcaster Borough Council. In January 1995, the council noted that there were rent arrears accruing on the rent account for the property. As a result of a visit to the premises, the housing officer spoke to Mr Turner. He stated that he had been living in the flat for over two years, initially as the Millers' lodger. For some time the Millers had been staying a lot with their son and eventually had left to live with him permanently in November 1994. The housing officer contacted the Millers at an address provided to him by Mr Turner and discovered this to be true. A notice to quit was served on the Millers dated 12 January 1995. The notice to quit in fact expired on 13 February 1995. As at the date of expiry the rent arrears stood at £660 and the contractual rent was £45 per week. The hearing of the possession action takes place on 13 June 1995.

Bradcaster Borough Council review their rents annually, and the rents are altered at the beginning of each fiscal year. In 1995, the new rents were to take effect from 4 April. If the council had let the property to a tenant at that date, the rent would have been increased to £50 per week. Mr Cooper made no payments to the council but refused to leave as he had no other place to go.

The council would be entitled to the following with regard to the money claimed:

1. against Mr and Mrs Miller – £660 arrears of rent;

2. against Mr Cooper – (a) damages for use and occupation of £815 (being seven weeks at £45 and a further ten weeks at £50); and (b) damages for use and occupation continuing at the rate of £50 per week until possession is delivered up.

Return date

In cases involving unlawful occupiers, where the occupier attends at the return date and raises a defence of the type discussed in this chapter, many housing officers find the experience frustrating for they are convinced that the occupier's assertions are unsubstantiated. Nevertheless, the possession list is not a time for lengthy argument or cross-examination. A defence of this nature, if it is to succeed, will certainly require discovery of the housing file relating to the property and so the issue will require more time than is allotted for the return date. In agreeing to an adjournment, no concession is being made about to the merits of the defendant's case. Directions should be sought forcing the defendant to provide a fully pleaded case as soon as possible. An *unless order* (see chapter 4, above) should be sought against the defendant requiring a defence by a certain date.

Nuisance and annoyance

Both the 1985 and 1988 Housing Acts include grounds for possession based upon nuisance and annoyance to neighbours or adjoining occupiers. In addition, most tenancy agreements will include an express term against committing acts of nuisance and annoyance, and so it will be possible to seek possession on the basis of a breach of a term of the tenancy agreement. (For a full discussion of the many facets to dealing with cases of this type see further S. Belgrave *Nuisance and Harassment*, Arden's Housing Library vol.3, 1995).

Nuisance cases involve difficult judgments for housing managers, involving the balancing of rights of tenants. Court cases involving neighbour disputes are notorious. They are often lengthy, and consequently very expensive and may achieve little. Housing managers will thus seek to avoid becoming embroiled in petty disputes between neighbours. The landlord cannot be forced by one tenant to take possession proceedings against another tenant unless it has expressly covenanted to do so in the tenancy agreement.

It is always possible for the tenants to bring court proceedings themselves for an injunction restraining the acts of nuisance. In addition, some social landlords operate a mediation service which allows the parties to come to a compromise and work towards conciliation. The issue of proceedings should only be used where considered absolutely necessary.

Nevertheless, there will be many instances where responsible landlords will feel that the interests of the majority of their tenants are best served by the eviction of an unruly household. Housing managers and officers have a crucial, and time consuming, role to play in the preparation of such a case. It is inherent in the concept of a nuisance that there must be a course of conduct. A period of monitoring is therefore required. Housing officers are in the awkward position of liaising between both the complainant(s) and the person alleged to have caused the nuisance.

The evidence of the commission of the acts of nuisance must come from the neighbours themselves. Housing officers cannot give evidence about the nuisance, only that complaints of a nuisance were made. These complaints are only hearsay evidence. Housing officers should provide the complainant with a nuisance diary and show him or her how to complete it. An explanation ought to be given about how important it is to keep the diary and the need for total co-operation in attending court if the proceedings are to go ahead. This may be difficult if the complainant is scared of the perpetrator of the nuisance.

The housing officer's evidence will be the key to the question of reasonableness, since the ground for possession is discretionary. The complainant may be able to give evidence of the tenant's reaction to being asked to stop the nuisance. How the defendant reacted towards the complainant, and whether or not the nuisance ceased as a consequence, will have a great bearing on the question of reasonableness. Many tenants, however, are unwilling to ask the complainant directly to cease the annoyance, preferring to ask the landlord to deal with the perpetrator. In any event, at trial, the defendant's attitude when confronted by the landlord's representative and his or her subsequent behaviour will be crucial. Housing officers must therefore keep detailed attendance notes of each meeting with the defendant.

Housing officers should consider other sources of evidence. At an early stage they need to contact other neighbours to see whether the effects of the nuisance are widespread, or if the complainant is overly sensitive or even the pursuit of a personal vendetta against the alleged perpetrator. If they confirm the complainant's version of events, then they too may be invited to give evidence. Conversely, if they do not have complaints, the case needs re-evaluation.

Local authority departments may have to be contacted in certain circumstances. Environmental health officers (EHOs) may be able to give valuable evidence about whether or not a nuisance is being caused, if the complaints concern activities which have a bearing on public health, eg harbouring of filth in the property, or keeping animals in inappropriate conditions. EHOs may also have suggestions about ways of abating the nuisance. For example, in a noise nuisance case where noise from stereo equipment is involved, an EHO may be may be able to give advice on arranging the stereo system so as to minimise the level of noise emanating from the building. Again, how the defendant reacts to any advice or warnings given by an environmental health officer will be relevant to the question of reasonableness. If the EHO is satisfied that there is a nuisance, an abatement notice may be served which could have bearings upon any subsequent case.

The nuisance may not be motivated by malice, or lack of consideration, but may be attributable to the inadequacy of the defendant. Someone who genuinely cannot look after the property, or who has difficulty in dealing with society, might reasonably be better accommodated in hostel accommodation where supervision and assistance is available. With the advent of care in the community this sort of situation is increasingly common for housing officers. Ideally, the problem should not arise at all, if in housing the vulnerable there is an appreciation of the need to provide appropriate housing and support services for such tenants. The involvement and evaluation of social services should be sought at an early opportunity.

Often problems are caused by the children of the tenant. In certain circumstances, action may be appropriate under the Children Act 1989. Sometimes cases involve young couples with children moving into communities where many of the residents are elderly and may have exercised the right to buy. Friction can develop between two age groups who have starkly contrasting life styles. Consideration must be given to the possibility that the complainants may unreasonably be objecting to someone viewed as different, who may even be used as a scapegoat for any problems in the community.

Witness statement

The housing officer's witness statement should address the following:

1. the tenancy agreement.

2. a description of the property and who lives in it. This is sometimes overlooked. In order to evaluate the complaints being made the court will need to know the layout of the houses or flats involved to see how many neighbours are affected by the alleged nuisance, and how many who one would expect to affected are not at court to give evidence. A basic sketch map showing who lives where may save a great deal of time at court.

3. the details of complaints made and the advice given to the complainant.

4. meetings with the defendant, including the warnings given and the defendant's reaction.

5. the involvement of environmental health services or social services if relevant.

6. the service of the notice seeking possession.

Return date

Even if the defendant does not attend court formal proof of the case will take some while and it may be useful to ensure that the court allots a longer period of time than would be usual for the case.

Undertakings

One useful alternative to pursuing the case is to invite the defendant to give an undertaking to the court. An *undertaking* is a formal promise to the court that the person giving the undertaking will not do certain things specified in the undertaking. Some defendants are unwilling to give an undertaking because they see it as a concession to the other side when they are adamant that they have done nothing wrong. It is important to realise that an undertaking is in no way an admission that anything untoward has occurred in the past. It is promise that nothing improper will happen in the future. See also Appendix.

The undertaking is given on court form N117. The defendant must read and sign this. The form bears the warning in bold type that if the undertaking is breached, the person making the undertaking may go to prison. This is because the breach of an undertaking is contempt of court. If the undertaking is subsequently breached the landlord may enforce it by applying to the court for *committal proceedings*. This involves proving to the court, beyond reasonable doubt, that the terms of the undertaking have been breached. If the court finds that there has been a breach of the undertaking it may punish the defendant with imprisonment or a fine.

The use of undertakings has its limitations. Complainants often find them unsatisfactory, as they are unconvinced that the nuisance will continue unless the defendant is evicted. The decision about whether or not to accept the undertaking is a matter for the landlord and not the complainants, however their views will inevitably be taken into account. No-one can force the defendant to give an undertaking, so it will not always be possible to resolve matters in this way. Moreover an undertaking can only be enforced by committal, and the standard of proof at such a hearing is at the higher standard of beyond reasonable doubt. It may be difficult to obtain sufficient evidence to satisfy the court to this standard.

On the other hand, when the undertaking is given the judge gives a stern and clear warning to the defendant about the consequences of failing to abide by the terms of the undertaking. Sometimes the formal nature of the court appearance has the desired effect and the tenant may finally realise the serious nature of continuing to be a nuisance. The possession action, meanwhile, is *adjourned with liberty* to restore. If the undertaking is honoured, the landlord has achieved the desired result without incurring the large costs of a full trial and has avoided the uncertainty of litigation. If the undertaking is breached, the possession action can be brought back to court and, if the ground is made out and it is shown that the defendant has breached the undertaking, the landlord's case is greatly strengthened on the issue of reasonableness, or, indeed, on the question of whether an outright rather than a suspended possession order is appropriate.

CHAPTER 9

LIMITED SECURITY

Assured shortholds / Accelerated possession procedure / Licensees / ***Summary possession***

This chapter considers the procedure for obtaining possession against two groups who have more limited security of tenure:

- assured shorthold tenants
- licensees.

Assured shortholds

Housing associations sometimes use assured shorthold tenancies for certain types of tenancy. An assured shorthold is a type of assured tenancy. It must be granted for a term of at least six months. Prior to the expiry of the term, the tenant has the same security of tenure as any other assured tenant and so possession can only be sought pursuant to the statutory grounds for possession. After the end of the fixed term, as long as a notice is served upon the tenant in the correct form, the tenant has no right to remain in the property.

Accelerated possession procedure

The county court now provides an accelerated possession procedure for claims against assured shorthold tenants. The one major drawback is that the procedure can only be used where the sole purpose of bringing proceedings is to gain possession, and so rent arrears cannot be claimed using this procedure. The application is made on a prescribed form (form N5A), and is accompanied by an affidavit. The form is self-explanatory, the purpose being to establish that the tenancy agreement is in the correct form and that a notice was served before the tenancy was entered into to the effect that the tenancy would be an assured shorthold, and that the appropriate notice determining the tenancy has been served. Once the tenant is served with the application, there is a period of 14 days in which to make a reply. Where the 14-day period expires without the defendant filing a reply, the landlord is entitled to file a written request with the court for an order for possession.

Licensees

In a number of cases the occupiers of local authority or housing association properties may only be licensees, this may be particularly true in the case of hostels (see further, A. Dymond, *Security of Tenure*, ch 10, Arden's Housing Library, vol.1, 1995). Once the licence to occupy has been terminated, the landlord has a choice whether to seek eviction through the normal procedure of issuing a summons for possession, or to use the accelerated fast-track procedure (which is normally used against squatters – see below).

Summary possession

Both the High Court and the county court provide a fast track procedure for the eviction of trespassers from land, commonly referred to as *summary possession proceedings*. The county court procedure is set out in CCR Order 24:

"Where a person claims possession of land which he alleges is occupied solely by a person or persons (not being a tenant or tenants holding over after the termination of the tenancy) who entered into or remained in occupation without his licence or consent or that of any predecessor in title of his, the proceedings may be brought by originating application in accordance with the provisions of this Order."

The procedure is available against squatters, but may also be used against licensees after the termination of the licence. It may also be used against unlawful subtenants after the tenancy comes to an end. It is not possible to claim damages for use and occupation under CCR Order 24.

Proceedings are initiated by an originating application, form N312, which must be supported by an affidavit. The application should state the names of the person against whom possession is sought, if they are known. The party making the application is called the *applicant* and the persons in occupation are referred to as the *respondents*.

Affidavit

There are three facts which must be stated in the affidavit:

1. The applicant's interest in the land must be defined. The affidavit should have proof of this interest exhibited to it. A freeholder should exhibit a land certificate, if the land is registered, or the conveyance passing title to the freeholder. A local authority in London which obtained title to land after the abolition of the Greater London Council is able to prove title by the production of the statutory instrument under which title passed.

2. The circumstances must be stated under which the land has been occupied without the applicant's licence or consent and in which the claim to possession arises. This will vary greatly from case to case. If possession is sought against former licensees, it must be shown that the licence has been properly determined. Otherwise, the officer will have to provide details of investigations which led to the discovery that there were trespassers on the land.

3. It must be stated that the applicant does not know the name of any person occupying the land who is not already named in the originating application. Order 24 proceedings may be commenced against *persons unknown* but if the applicant does know the name of an occupier, that must be included in the originating application. There is an important difference between the requirements for service of an application upon a named respondent, and on persons unknown (see below).

As with all affidavits, it may contain statements of information or belief (hearsay). The sources of such information must be identified.

Service on named respondent

Any person named in the application must be served – in one of the following ways – with (a) the application, (b) the affidavit in support, and (c) a notice of the return day in one of the following ways:

1. by delivering the documents to the respondent personally;

2. by an officer of the court leaving the documents or sending them to the respondent at the property;

3. if the respondent is represented by solicitors, and a certificate to that effect has been filed with the court, by service on the solicitor; or

4. by any other method which the court may direct.

Service on unknown persons

Where possession is sought against persons unknown, the application and other documents must also be served, unless the court directs otherwise, in one of the following ways:

1. The documents may be affixed to the main door or another conspicuous part of the property, and, if practicable, posted through the letter box enclosed in a sealed envelope addressed to "the occupiers";

2. Where there is no building, sealed transparent envelopes containing the documents addressed to "the occupiers" may be affixed to stakes which are placed in the ground on conspicuous parts of the land. The stakes and the envelopes are provided for the court by the applicant.

Failure to provide proper service will not nullify the proceedings totally, but it is important to ensure that service is correct, for the aim of summary possession proceedings is to gain possession quickly and, if there is a mistake as to service, the matter will usually be adjourned for proper service. If all the occupiers attend the court however, and have thus suffered no prejudice as a consequence of the mistake, the court is entitled to proceed on the basis of the defective service.

In the case of residential property, service must be effected not less than five days before the hearing, unless it is an urgent case when a court may give leave for only two clear days. The application to abridge the time for service may be made at the hearing itself. Any day on which the court is closed is not included in this calculation.

The hearing

The hearing is before a judge or district judge. As with any return date, only a short time will have been allotted. The applicant has to satisfy the court that service has been correctly effected. If the judge is then satisfied about the affidavit in support, the burden is placed upon the occupier to establish that he or she has some right to remain in the property.

If the occupier is able to raise a defence which will require a full hearing, then the matter may be adjourned to allow a proper trial. A court faced with a respondent who has not had the benefit of legal advice but who appears to have an arguable defence will usually be granted an adjournment. An order concerning any directions will be made – and should be made if the issues are complicated – and the rival contentions should best be set out in formal pleadings. The initial hearing is not, however, confined to affidavit evidence and, if time permits, the court may still hear oral evidence and full legal argument. Accordingly, the officer who provided the affidavit must be in attendance at the hearing.

The order

In proceedings against occupiers who entered the property unlawfully, ie without the applicant's permission, the court has no discretion to postpone the order for possession. The order will be for possession forthwith. No claim for damages for use and occu-pation can be made in Order 24 proceedings, but the applicant is not prevented from making a separate claim in separate proceedings.

PART III

POSSESSION PROCEDURE: ORDERS AND FURTHER ACTION

CHAPTER 10

POSSESSION ORDERS

Immediate order / Outright order / Suspended possession order / Order not to be enforced without the leave / Money judgment / Consent order / Costs /

Types of order / Costs orders at the return date / Legal aid

As has already been discussed, a successful landlord is not guaranteed an outright possession order. Possession orders fall into three types: immediate, outright and suspended, each of which will be discussed in this chapter, together with a number of other orders which the court may grant, including those relating to costs.

Immediate order

An immediate order for possession means that possession is granted to the landlord straightaway. The only delay involved is occasioned by obtaining a warrant for possession from the court, and a subsequent notice of appointment from the bailiffs. Such an order will be granted to a successful applicant in summary possession proceedings, see chapter 9.

Outright order

An outright order for possession grants the landlord possession on a specified day. The position at common law was that the judge had the discretion to allow the occupier a reasonable time before the order took effect. In the county court, the court's discretion is limited by section 89 of the Housing Act 1980. The basic rule is that the possession order must now take effect no more than 14 days after the day of the hearing unless it would cause the occupier exceptional hardship, in which case the court may extend the period up to six weeks. There is no clear guidance about what would constitute exceptional hardship, but logically something over and above the normal consequences of homelessness must be required. The court might be expected to exercise the extended discretion if the tenant or a member of the family is ill or pregnant.

Significantly, the restriction on the court's discretion does not apply where the court had the power to make the order for possession only if it considered it reasonable to make an order (section 89(2)(c) of the Housing Act 1980).

To sum up:

- Where possession is obtained under a mandatory

ground of the Housing Act 1988 (Grounds 1 to 8), or against an assured shorthold tenant, or against a tenant who does not have security of tenure under either the Housing Act 1985 or the Housing Act 1988, the court must make an order taking effect within the next 14 days, unless there is exceptional hardship – in which case the discretion is extended to six weeks.

- Where possession is obtained under a discretionary ground, under whichever Act, the court has a wide discretion to postpone or even suspend the order.

Suspended possession order

Where possession is sought against a tenant under a discretionary ground, the order for possession may be suspended on terms, in which case the landlord will not be able to enforce the possession order until the tenant has breached the terms of suspension. Such an order is particularly common in rent arrears cases, where the order is suspended on terms that the defendant pays the current rent plus a certain amount off the arrears of rent each week or month.

The court's discretion is not limited in this regard, and any reasonable terms may be enforced. Thus a suspended order may be useful in a case brought on the basis of nuisance and annoyance to neighbours. As long as no further acts of nuisance are committed by the tenant, the order cannot be enforced. Great care must be taken in drafting the terms of such an order, so that it is entirely clear to both parties what behaviour has to be curtailed.

Order not to be enforced without the leave

Once a term of the order has been breached, the landlord is entitled to enforce the order. This is done by an application for a warrant for possession, which does not involve a court hearing and can be done with no forewarning to the tenant. In a rent arrears case, this ought not present problems as it should be clear whether or not the money has been paid.

Where the terms are more complicated – as in a case involving nuisance – the court may be unwilling to leave the decision about when the order may be enforced to the landlord. This is because what conduct constitutes a nuisance is inevitably a decision of fact and degree in each case. The court may, accordingly, impose the condition that the order cannot be enforced without the leave (permission) of the court so that, before a request for a warrant is made, an application to the court must be made.

Money judgment

If the order includes a money judgment, eg for arrears of rent, a date by which the money should be paid may be included. Where no time is specified, the payment is deemed to be due in 14 days.

Consent order

It is quite common in possession cases for the tenant to agree to the order which is to be made, eg to an order suspended on repayment of arrears at a certain rate per week. Because of the statutory restrictions in the Housing Acts 1985 and 1988 on the power of the court to make an order for possession it has been held that a consent order cannot be made by the court, unless either there is an investigation of the facts or an admission by the defendant of the truth of the facts.

Case report

Mr Fadayomi was the secure tenant of a flat owned by the London Borough of Wandsworth. The authority wished to obtain possession on the basis that they required possession in order to carry out works to the flat (Ground 10, Schedule 2, Housing Act 1985). In order for possession to be obtained under that Ground suitable alternative accommodation must be offered to the tenant. A number of offers were made to Mr Fadayomi and, since his marriage had broken down, separate offers were made to his wife. All offers were refused.

A consent order was made on Mr Fadayomi's undertaking that his wife and children would be allowed to live at the alternative accommodation which was on offer at the time of trial. Mrs Fadayomi sought to object to the order, through a letter from her solicitors. The judge refused to consider the letter, as the solicitors were not officially on the court record, as legal aid had not been issued.

Mrs Fadayomi successfully sought to have the order quashed in the Court of Appeal. The Court found that since there had been no express admission of the facts, nor investigation of them, the judge had no jurisdiction to grant the order. Furthermore, as a member of the family, Mrs Fadayomi had an

interest in the issue of alternative accommodation and the right to present her case on this issue.
London Borough of Wandsworth v Fadayomi (1987) 19 HLR 512, CA.

In some circumstances, however, the court will be willing to imply that the tenant has admitted the facts, which allow the making of the order.

Case report
Mr Bruce sought to exercise the right to buy the house let to him by Worthing Borough Council. On investigation, the council concluded that the house was not occupied by Mr Bruce as his only or principal home. They refused the application. Mr Bruce sought a declaration in the county court that he was a secure tenant. The council counterclaimed for possession of the house on the basis of non-occupation and arrears of rent.

When the matter came to court some evidence was heard but the case was then settled on the basis that the council would not pursue their money claim but the applicant would give up possession. Part of the consent order declared that the "plaintiff's [Mr Bruce's] claim be dismissed."

Mr Bruce sought to have the order set aside on the basis that no specific findings of fact as to his status had been made and accordingly the judge had no jurisdiction to make the order. In the Court of Appeal, it was held that even if there was no express admission of the fact that he was not a secure tenant in the order, it could be implied and that this was sufficient in the circumstances.
Bruce v Worthing Borough Council (1993) 26 HLR 223, CA

Thus where an order is being made by consent it is important that it includes express admissions by the tenant that, eg there are arrears of rent or that it is not occupied as his or her only or principal home. While the courts have been willing to approach the matter on a common sense basis as in the *Bruce* case, it is always advisable to take great care before agreeing a consent order.

Costs

The basic principle is that the party who wins an action is entitled to his or her costs. Nevertheless, costs are entirely in the discretion of the court and the winning party need not be awarded their costs.

Case report

Mr Ottway sought possession against his tenant Mr Jones on the ground that he had been a nuisance and annoyance. The last act of nuisance complained of took place in June. Proceedings commenced in October and the case was heard the following March. The judge found that the conduct complained of amounted to a nuisance but, having regard to all the circumstances of the case – in particular, the fact that no further instances of nuisance had occurred since June and the grave effect on the tenant's household and family – he decided that it was not reasonable to make an order for possession. Nevertheless, he ordered Mr Jones to pay Mr Ottway's costs. The Court of Appeal refused an appeal against the order on costs. Admittedly, it was unusual for a party (the tenant in this case) who won a case to be ordered to

pay the other side's costs, but the judge had not been wrong to exercise his discretion as he did. The incidents of nuisance were very unpleasant, involving drunken and vulgar behaviour. When the landlord commenced the action he had no guarantee that the behaviour would cease.
Ottway v Jones [1955] 2 All ER 585 CA.

Types of costs order

The following are the common orders relating to costs which are made by the court. They indicate who will bear the costs of a particular action.

Costs in interlocutory matters

A party who wins the trial may not get all the costs incurred in fighting the action. Prior to the trial itself there may have been a number of hearings concerning the procedure of the case. Such hearings are called *interlocutory*. A party who is successful at trial may still have to pay for costs incurred at an interlocutory hearing.

The following list of costs orders covers those which may be made at the final hearing and those at interlocutory hearings.

Costs: this entitles the specified party to have its costs paid by the other party.

No order as to costs: this means that each party bears its own costs for the hearing.

Costs reserved: the costs of the hearing will be dealt with on a subsequent occasion. Unless otherwise specified the party who eventually wins the action will be awarded the costs for the earlier hearing.

Costs in the cause: The party who is eventually successful in the action will get the costs of the earlier hearing.

Costs in any event: The party in whose favour this order is made will be entitled to his or her costs for that hearing whatever the result of the action as a whole.

Plaintiff's costs in cause: The plaintiff's costs of the hearing will have to be borne by the party who loses the action as a whole, but the plaintiff will not have to pay the defendant's costs of the hearing whatever the final result of the trial.

Defendant's costs in cause: This is the reverse of "plaintiff's costs in cause". The defendant's costs of the hearing will have to be borne by the party who ultimately loses the action, but the defendant will not have to pay the plaintiff's costs of the hearing whatever the final result of the trial.

Costs assessed: Commonly where possession is ordered at the return date the judge will assess the landlord's costs. A figure in the region of £175 is the amount generally awarded if the landlord has been represented.

Costs to be taxed if not agreed: Where the matter proceeds to a full trial the calculation of the parties costs is too complicated to be dealt with by the judge at the end of the trial. The parties may subsequently agree on the costs, or they may submit them to a district judge who will decide whether items included have been properly incurred. This is called taxation.

Costs not to be enforced without the leave of the court: If an unsuccessful party is legally aided, then the costs order will not be enforced against the party without the leave of the court (which may subsequently be sought if the unsuccessful party's financial circumstances improve).

Costs orders at the return date

Housing managers and officers who present possession actions themselves must be aware of the full range of orders available. Certain orders are particularly useful if the matter proceeds beyond the return date. If the tenant or occupier attends the hearing and raises a defence for the first time, assuming that the defence appears to have merit, the judge will probably adjourn the case and give directions. In these circumstances, the housing manager or officer should ask the judge that the defendant pay the plaintiff's costs *in any event* so that even if the landlord eventually loses the case it will not have to pay the costs of the return date, which should have been avoided if the defendant had acted promptly and replied to the summons. Some judges are unwilling to make such an order at a return date. The second best order as to costs in such a situation is *plaintiff's costs in the cause.*

If a landlord successfully obtains an order for possession at the return date, then the landlord will generally be awarded costs.

Legal aid

A defendant who is on income support, or who is on a low income, may be entitled to legal aid (ie financial assistance from the state) to defend a possession action. Apart from the income criterion, in order to qualify for legal aid the defendant has to have a reasonable prospect of defending the case successfully.

The grant of legal aid has significant implications for the landlord bringing the action. Even if the landlord is successful and is granted possession at the end of the trial, the landlord generally will not recover its costs from the defendant. A successful landlord will be awarded its costs, but the court will add the proviso that the order "is not to be enforced without the leave of the court". Effectively, the landlord is left unable to recover its costs unless the defendant's financial standing subsequently improves, at which point (if it hears about the change of circumstances) the landlord is able to return to court to ask that the restriction imposed by the court be removed. The successful party has six years after the judgment was made in which to make such an application.

CHAPTER 11

FURTHER ACTION

Warrants for possession / Appeals / Stay of execution / Setting aside an order for possession / Subsequent conduct by parties

Even after a final possession order has been made further legal processes may be required to secure compliance with the order, in particular seeking and executing a warrant for possession. Parties may seek to appeal the order, and defendants – especially those who did not attend the original hearing – may seek to have orders set aside. These procedures are considered in this chapter. Finally, the chapter considers when a new tenancy may be created, notwithstanding the fact that an outright possession order has been obtained.

Warrants for possession

An order for possession may only be enforced by a warrant of possession. Any attempt by the landlord to evict the tenant without the use of a warrant is likely to result in a claim by the tenant for unlawful eviction.

The landlord wishing to enforce a possession order is entitled to apply for a warrant the day after the court specified in the order that the tenant should deliver possession up to the landlord. Thus, if a judge orders "possession in 14 days", on the fifteenth day the landlord is entitled to go to the court to ask for a warrant for possession to be issued. The issue of a warrant is an administrative process. There is no hearing and the landlord does not have to notify the tenant that a warrant is to be issued. The exception to this is if the court made it a term of the order that no warrant is to be issued without the leave of the court.

If the order for possession was suspended on terms, then the landlord is entitled to apply for a warrant once the terms of the order are breached. This would occur as soon as a tenant against whom an order suspended on terms – say, the payment of the current rent plus a certain amount off the arrears each week – fails to pay the required sum.

A request for a warrant is made on a standard court form (form N325). It remains in force for one year. After that period of time it will be necessary to seek the leave of the court to have the warrant renewed. Such an application may be made by writing to the court setting out the reasons for delay.

After the warrant is issued, the landlord is informed of the time when the bailiff will call at the property to execute the warrant. This may be some weeks after the request for the warrant. In effect, a tenant against whom a possession order has been made has a period of grace in addition to that which may have been awarded by the court.

Appeals

The party which loses at the trial may be allowed to appeal the order made. A losing party may appeal **as of right** from the district judge to a judge. The appeal is not a retrial and it is therefore necessary for the appellant to show that the district judge made a mistake as to the law. The judge in such circumstances is exercising similar powers to those of the Court of Appeal, when an appeal is made to them from a judge (see below). The appeal must be made on notice which must be served within 14 days after the day on which judgment was given.

Appeals from a judge are made to the Court of Appeal. Such an appeal is not by way of rehearing. The Court of Appeal are bound to accept the factual findings of the judge at the trial (unless the judge's findings were plainly irrational). Appeals to the Court of Appeal are thus confined to cases where the judge has made a mistake on the law. With regard to actions based on discretionary grounds for possession, the Court of Appeal has emphasised that it will rarely interfere with a decision of a trial judge on the issue of reasonableness. The judge's finding in this regard would have to have taken into account factors which were irrelevant, or not taken into account factors which were relevant, for the result to be challenged. If the judge has taken into account all the right considerations, but come to a surprising decision, it is hard to appeal.

The party wishing to appeal a decision in a possession action must ask for *leave to appeal* from the trial judge. If the judge refuses leave, the aggrieved party may still apply to the Court of Appeal itself for leave. If leave is given, the notice of appeal must be served not later than four weeks after the day on which the order was sealed.

Stay of execution

Even though a warrant may have been issued, the tenant – or the tenant's spouse – still has the opportunity to apply to the court to suspend the execution of the warrant. Section 85(2) of the Housing Act 1985, and section 9(2) of the Housing Act 1988, provide the court with the power to suspend the warrant for possession on terms. An application for a stay of execution is made on court forms N244 or N245 and should be supported by an affidavit. The application can be made at any time before the warrant is executed by the bailiffs.

In a case based upon rent arrears – whether the tenant is secure or assured – if the court decides to suspend or postpone the execution of the warrant, it must impose conditions regarding payment of arrears – unless this would cause exceptional hardship to the tenant, or would otherwise be unreasonable. The court may also impose any other conditions it may think fit. The contractual tenant's spouse has the same rights as the tenant, if the spouse is residing in the property. This ceases to be the case once, following divorce proceedings, a decree absolute is made and the marriage is ended.

Setting aside an order for possession

Even after the warrant has been executed, it is still possible for the tenant to apply to set aside the possession order or, indeed, for someone who was not a party to the action to apply to be joined to the action and argue a right to remain in the dwelling. The tenant, or other occupier, must be able to show that there was an arguable defence to the action if the order is to be set aside. It will also be necessary for the defendant to show that the case falls within one of the limited circumstances in which the court allows an order to be set aside.

By far the most common situation is that in which the tenant was not present at the hearing (CCR Order 37 rule 2). A defendant will have to explain why he or she was not present because someone who simply chose not to attend the hearing will not be entitled to have the order set aside. A defendant who was ill or otherwise unable to come to court will have a good excuse. Likewise, where the defendant was unaware of the proceedings because they did not arrive through the post, the defendant may be entitled to have the order set aside (CCR Order 37 rule 3).

It is also possible for the defendant to apply for a rehearing of the action before the judge who made the order. This may be done where there was misconduct on the plaintiff's behalf or where fresh evidence has come to light which could not have been available at the trial (CCR Order 37 rule 1). An application for a rehearing must be made within 14 days of the trial, but an application to extend time may be made under CCR Order 13 rule 4 if that time limit has expired.

Subsequent conduct by parties

Housing officers should take care to ensure that the landlord's dealings with a tenant against whom a possession order is made do not create a new tenancy. This is of particular importance in the context of secure tenancies.

A secure tenancy ends on the date on which the tenant is to give up possession in pursuance of the order (section 82(2) Housing Act 1985). When the terms of a possession order are breached, the secure tenant becomes a trespasser and the landlord can enforce the order by a warrant. Nevertheless, the tenant could still apply to suspend the warrant on terms. Most social landlords do not enforce a possession order immediately if there is a minor or explicable breach. Indeed, housing managers will probably have to report the case to a committee who will have to make the ultimate decision as to whether or not to issue a warrant. As a result, there is a delay between the default and the issue of the warrant.

During this delay, the occupier may well make payments to the landlord. The difficulty is that if the occupier is a trespasser as soon as he or she breaches the order, and the occupier then makes payments to the landlord, it might be argued that this shows that a new tenancy has been created. It is thought that the circumstances in which such an argument would be successful will be rare. Much will turn on the facts of each case. Nevertheless, care should be taken to inform a secure tenant who breaches a suspended order that there is no intention to create a new tenancy and action should be taken swiftly once the tenant defaults.

Some landlords have also been known to use a policy of obtaining outright orders for possession but allowing the tenant to remain in possession, notwithstanding that the possession date has passed, provided that rent payments are maintained. Those landlords using this policy argue that an outright order has more "effect" on tenants than a suspended one. There is, however, a much greater danger in these circumstances that the court will find that by acceptance of rent – after the date for possession – a new tenancy has been created.

Case report

In 1984 the London Borough of Brent granted a secure tenancy to Mr and Mrs Burrows. In 1986 Mr Burrows left. Mrs Burrows fell into considerable arrears of rent. The council obtained an outright order for possession against her, and judgment for over £2,000 rent arrears. Before the time for possession and payment arrived, the council entered into an agreement whereby Mrs Burrows could continue to live in the flat provided that she paid a sum equivalent to the rent and a sum off the arrears. The payments were documented as rent, and notices of increase in rent were served. Mrs Burrows subsequently failed to comply with the agreement. The council issued a warrant for possession. It was argued for Mrs Burrows that the effect of the agreement was to create a new tenancy. The county court found that a new tenancy had been created, and the Court of Appeal upheld that decision.

Burrows v Brent LBC (1995) 27 HLR 748, CA.

PART IV

APPENDIX:

SPECIMEN FORMS
GLOSSARY OF TERMS

Form N5
Summons for possession

The Plaintiff (your landlord or mortgage lender) is claiming possession of 10 Barholme Court, Ainsworthy Road, Sheffchester for the reasons in the attached particulars of claim.

The Plaintiff is also making a claim for money (details are given in the particulars of claim).

What this means

• On the date set out below, the court will decide whether or not you have to leave and, if you have to leave, when.

What you should do

• Get help and advice immediately from a solicitor or any of the advice agencies on the attached list.

• Make sure the court knows as much about your circumstances as possible by:

• filling in the reply form attached to this summons, and

• coming to the hearing

(The notes on the back of this form give you more information about what you should do.)

The court will make its decision on 4th October 1995 at 10.30 am at Sheffchester County Court, 56 The Mall, Sheffchester.

Form N119
Particulars of claim: Rent arrears

Particulars of claim for possession
(rented property)

In the Sheffchester County Court
Case No.S456834

Plaintiff
The Mayor and Burgesses of Sheffchester Borough Council

Defendants
(1) Arthur Thomas Jackson
(2) Muriel Jane Jackson

About the tenancy
1.(a) The Plaintiff has a right to possession of the property at 10 Barholme Court, Ainsworthy Road, Sheffchester.
(b) The property is a dwelling-house.

2.(a) The property is let the Defendants under a secure tenancy agreement which began on 9th November 1991. The rent is £78 per week payable weekly in advance.
(b) The daily rate at which any unpaid rent should be calculated is £11.14 per day.

3. The reason the Plaintiff is asking for possession is:
(a) because the rent has not been paid as it should have under the terms of the tenancy agreement.

Details are set out below.
£1,067 rent is outstanding up the date hereof. Only one payment of £45 has been made during the period of 18 weeks prior to the date hereof. See Schedule A attached hereto showing a full printout of the rent account.
(b) because the Defendants have failed to comply with the terms of the tenancy agreement in the following way: *Not applicable.*

4. The following steps have already been taken to recover the arrears:
By letters dated 3rd March 1995, and 29th March 1995, the Plaintiff wrote to the Defendants requiring payment of the outstanding arrears. A housing officer in the employment of the Plaintiff met the second Defendant on 5th June 1995 and an agreement was reached that the Defendant would pay the current rent plus £5 per week off the rent arrears. The Defendants failed to keep to this agreement and have failed to contact the Plaintiff despite subsequent requests from the Plaintiff by letter.

5. The appropriate notice seeking possession was served on the Defendant on 1st July 1995.

About the Defendants
6. The following information is known about the Defendants. So far as the Plaintiff is aware, the first Defendant is a self employed carpenter. The second Defendant is not in employment. The Defendants have failed to respond to requests for

meetings following the Defendants' failure to keep to the aforementioned meetings. No payments are made directly by the Department of Social Security to the Plaintiff.

About the Plaintiff

7. The Plaintiff is asking the court to take the following information into account when making its decision whether or not to grant an order for possession.

The Plaintiff is a local housing authority. The Defendant has consistently been in arrears of rent over the past 2 years, paying lump sums periodically in reduction of the arrears. Efforts have been made by the Plaintiff to reach an agreement as to the payment of arrears but the Defendants have refused to make contact.

What the court is being asked to do

8. The Plaintiff is asking the court to make an order that the Defendants:

(a) give the Plaintiff possession of the property mentioned in paragraph 1;

(b) pay the unpaid rent due from 12th February 1995 to the date of issue of this summons, and from the date of the summons to the date an order is made, at the rate of £78 per week;

(c) pay the costs of making this application for possession.

9. The Plaintiff is also asking that judgment is entered against the Defendants for the total amount of arrears outstanding up to the time an order is made and costs.

Signed: Colin Ward
Sheffchester Borough Council Legal Department

Address where notices about this case can be sent:

Sheffchester Borough Council
Legal Services Department
The Town Hall
High Road
Sheffchester

Form N117
Undertaking

In the Sheffchester County Court
Between
Sheffchester Borough Council
and
David William Bolt

On the 12th day of May 1995, David William Bolt was represented by counsel and gave an undertaking to the court promising
(1) not to play or permit to be played any stereo system or musical instrument in the premises known as 10 Craft Lane, Sheffchester so as to be audible outside the said premises;
(2) not to assault, threaten or in any way interfere with John Christopher Davis whether by himself or encouraging or instructing others;

And to be bound by these promises until further order of the court.

The court explained to the Defendant the meaning of the undertaking and the consequences of failing to keep his promises;
And the court accepted his undertaking;
And the court ordered that:
(1) the matter be adjourned generally liberty to restore;
(2) costs reserved.

Dated ....

To David William Bolt of 10 Craft Lane, Sheffchester.

You may be sent to prison if you break the promises that you have given to this court.

I understand the undertaking that I have given, and that if I break any of my promises to the Court I may be sent to prison for contempt of court.

Signed:

Form N26
Order for possession (Assured tenancies)

In the Sheffchester County Court
Case No.S980768

Marine Housing Association

and

Mark Trevor Andrewes

To the Defendant

1. The court has decided that you should give the Plaintiff possession of 41 Ilsham Road, Sheffchester. This means you must leave the property on 8th August 1995.

2. You must also pay the Plaintiff's costs of making the application for possession. You must pay
(a) £250 to the Plaintiff on or before 8th August 1995.
(b) £ . . . . to the Plaintiff by instalments of £ . . . . per . . . . The first instalment to be paid on or before . . . .

3. Payments should be made to the Plaintiff at the address given on the front of the application for possession.

4. If you do not leave the property and pay the costs by the dates given, the Plaintiff can ask the court bailiff to evict you and remove sufficient of

your goods to pay the costs. This is called "enforcing the order and money judgment".

Dated 25th July 1995.

Form N26
Order for possession
(possession suspended) (rented property)

In the Sheffchester County Court
Case No.S123467

Sheffchester Borough Council

and

David Edward Bilton
Karen Lillian Bilton

To the Defendants
1. The court has decided that unless you make the payments as set out in paragraph 3 you must give the Plaintiff possession of 45 Maltby Square, Sheffchester on 22nd August 1995.

2. You must also pay to the Plaintiff £890 for unpaid rent, use and occupation of the property and
(a) £175 for the Plaintiff's costs of making the application for possession.
(b) the Plaintiff's costs to be taxed on scale . . . .
If the Plaintiff's costs are to be taxed, that is looked at by a judge to decide if they are reasonable you will have to pay those costs within 14 days of taxation. You will be sent a copy of the Plaintiff's bill and will be able to object to any amounts in it. The judge will decide if your objections are valid.

3. You must pay the Plaintiff the total amount of £1,065 by instalments of £7.50 per week in addition to the current rent. The current rent is £45 per week. The first payment of both these amounts must be made on or before 15th August 1995. When you have paid the total amount mentioned, the Plaintiff will not be able to take any steps to evict you as a result of this order.

4. If you do not pay the money owed and costs by the dates given and the current rent, the Plaintiff can ask the court bailiff to evict you and remove your goods to obtain payment. This is called "enforcing the order and money judgment".

5. Payments should be made to the Plaintiff at the place where you would normally pay your rent. If you need more information about making payments you should contact the Plaintiff. The court cannot accept any payments.

Dated 8th August 1995

GLOSSARY OF TERMS

This glossary provides a concise explanation of the meaning of some of the more legalistic and technical terms used in the guide.

Affidavit
– a formal written statement by a witness made on oath.

Assured tenancy
– a tenancy that fulfils the requirements of the Housing Act 1988. An assured tenancy can be granted only from 15 January 1989 by landlords who are either housing associations or in the private sector.

Burden of proof
– the obligation on a party to prove a fact in issue between the parties. The burden of proof in civil proceedings is "on the balance of probabilities".

Committal proceedings
– proceedings brought by one party to enforce the breach by the other of the terms of an injunction or undertaking.

Consolidation
– the hearing together of two separate cases which share common issues which are to be decided between the parties.

Covenant
– a clause in a tenancy agreement under which either the landlord or the tenant promises to act in a certain way; for example, to carry out repairs or not to be a nuisance to neighbours.

Cross-examination
– the questioning of a witness by the opposing party.

Directions
– an order by the court setting out the procedural steps which are to be gone through prior to the trial of a case, and providing a time scale within which the steps are to be carried out.

Discovery
– the production by each party of all documents which may be relevant to the issues of the case.

Evidence in chief
– the evidence given by a witness in support of the case to be made.

Ex parte
– an application to the court which is made urgently and without the opposing party in the litigation being informed that the hearing is to take place. (Abbreviation: *ex p.*)

Fixed term tenancy
– a tenancy which is granted for a fixed period, for example, six months, or one year, or 99 years. (Compare periodic tenancy, below.)

Further and better particulars
– if alleged facts set out in a pleading are too general, a request by the opposing party may be made to expand on those allegations in a formal request for further and

better particulars. (See also pleadings, below.)

Hearsay
– an out of court statement tendered in court as evidence of the truth of its contents. Hearsay is essentially "second-hand" evidence.

Injunction
– an order of the court that a person should carry out certain acts or should refrain from carrying out certain acts.

Informal admission
– a statement by a party which contradicts a fact relied upon in support of his or her case.

Interlocutory
– an interim order in a case that is made before the final trial and judgment, most often used with injunctions.

Interrogatories
– formal questions put by one party designed to elicit statements of fact from the opposing party. Interrogatories are answered by affidavit.

Leading question
– a question asked of a witness which implies the answer, Yes or No.

Notice seeking possession
– the notice served by the landlord on a secure or assured tenancy prior to commencing possession proceedings. It must specify the grounds on which possession is sought against the tenant.

Notice to quit
– formal notice by a landlord determining a periodic tenancy of a tenant who does not have security of tenure.

Nuisance
– the interference by one occupier of land with other's occupation of their own land.

Particulars of claim
– the formal statement of the plaintiff's case which must be served with the summons for possession.

Periodic tenancy
– a tenancy which does not have a fixed time-span from the outset but which is set in terms of a regular rental payment, for example, monthly or weekly.

Plaintiff
– the person bringing the case, which in possession proceedings will be the landlord.

Pleadings
– the formal statements to the court by each party of the facts of the case upon which they intend to rely at trial.

Quiet enjoyment
– the right of tenants to occupy their homes without interference from their landlords. A right to quiet enjoyment is automatically implied into all tenancy agreements.

Re-examination
– questions by the party who called a witness in response to matters arising out of cross-examination.

Return date

– the date set by the court for the hearing of a summons for possession.

Secure tenancy

– a tenancy that fulfils the requirements of the Housing Act 1985, granted by local authorities or, before 15 January 1989, housing associations.

Summons

– the document issued by the county court which commences the action.

Unless order

– an order of the court requiring a party to proceedings to act within a certain time. It includes the provision that if the act is not carried out, the party will be prevented from continuing to pursue or defend the case.

Unauthorised occupier

– the term often used to describe a trespasser who entered property lawfully. An example would be a guest of the tenant who no longer has any right to remain in the property.

Undertaking

– a formal promise to the court to perform or cease a specified act.

Witnesses statements

– written statements by the trial witnesses setting out all the facts concerned in the evidence which they are to give in court. The statements are exchanged by the parties in advance of the trial.

CUMULATIVE INDEX

Abandoned premises
- conditions for security of tenure, 1:53-54
- notice to quit, 1:110-111

Absence from premises
- conditions for security of tenure, 1:48-49
- prolonged, 1:48-49

Accelerated procedure
- possession proceedings, 1:108, **4:114**

Accident
- inevitable, as defence to private nuisance action, 3:21-22

Accommodation
- disabled, for, 1:80
- elderly, for, 1:19-20
- employment related, 1:76-77, **4:41-42**
- essential for job, 1:24-25
- homeless persons, for 1:34-35, 1:42
- hostel. *See* Hostel accommodation
- information about applications, 2:58-59
- job mobility, 1:35-36
- pending works, 1:37, 1:77-78, **4:40-41**
- shared, 1:45-46
- sheltered, 1:81
- special needs, 1:80-81
- tied, 1:24, 1:88, **4:34-35**

Adjournment of possession proceedings. *See* Possession proceedings

Affidavit
- evidence, **4:71-72**
- meaning, **4:154**
- summary possession, **4:116**

Agreement
- surrender, to, 1:125
- tenancy,
  - assured tenancy, 2:54-55
  - breach of, as ground for possession, 3:60-61
  - changing terms of, 2:50-55
  - covenant, meaning, 2:99
  - fixed term tenancy, 2:54
  - harassment, prevention of, 3:84-87
  - periodic tenancy, 2:54-55
  - secure tenancy, 2:50-54,
  - termination of, **4:8-13**

Agricultural holdings
- tenancy of, 1:37, 1:40

Agricultural land
- assured tenancy, exception to, 1:40

Allocation of housing
- information about, 2:57-58
- secure tenants, information to, 2:62
- suitable alternative accommodation, 1:91-92

Ancillary rights of tenants
- summary, 2:3-4

Animals
- private nuisance, as, 3:16

Annoyance
- assured tenant, grounds for possession against, 1:88
- evidence, 1:72
- letter to tenant causing, 1:133
- meaning, 1:71
- neighbours, complaints from, 1:72
- nuisance and, 3:61-63
- possession proceedings,
  - generally, **4:106-109**
  - proof of annoyance, **4:39**
  - return date, **4:110**

Annoyance – *cont*
possession proceedings – *cont*
undertakings, **4:110-112**
witness statement, **4:110**
secure tenant, grounds for possession against, 1:70-73
those who live with tenant, caused by, 1:71
visitors, caused by, 1:71
Appeals
possession procedure, **4:136-137**
Application to set aside possession order, 1:123-124
Assignment
assured tenancy, of, 2:44-46
enforcement of right of, 2:28-29
exchange, by way of,
consent, grounds for refusing, 2:36-39
generally, 2:35
landlord's written consent, 2:35-36
generally, 1:8, 2:31
potential successor, to, 2:32-33
proof of, 2:33-34
secure tenancy, of,
exchange, assignment by way of, 2:35-39
generally, 2:32
mutual exchange, 2:35-39
potential successor, to, 2:32-33
proof of assignment, 2:33-34
property transfer order, 2:32
successor assignee, seeking possession against, 2:34-35
statutory periodic tenancy, 2:46
Assured shorthold tenancy
county court, accelerated procedure in, 1:108
features, 1:106-107
hostel accommodation, 1:116
nature of, 1:105
new shorthold, 1:107
possession, 1:107, **4:113-114**
probationary tenancy, 3:44-45
purposes, 1:106
Assured tenancy
assignment of, 2:44-2:46
change of landlord, 1:42
conditions, 1:44
consultation with assured tenants, 2:75-77
exceptions,
agricultural holdings, tenancy of, 1:40
agricultural land, tenancy of, 1:40
business tenancy, 1:40
Crown tenancy, 1:41
exempt landlord, 1:41
high rateable values, tenancy of premises with, 1:39
holiday lets, 1:40
homeless person, 1:42
licensed premises, 1:40
long leaseholder, 1:40
resident landlord, 1:41
student lets, 1:40
tenancy created before commencement of Act, 1:39
tenants with other classes of protection, 1:41
forfeiture of, 1:66
generally, 1:29
lodgers, 2:47
meaning, 2:99, 3:99, **4:154**
nature of, 1:38-39
possession, grounds of,
annoyance, 1:88
breach of term of tenancy, 1:87
deterioration of dwelling-house, 1:88

Assured tenancy – *cont*
possession, grounds of – *cont*
discretionary grounds, 1:86-88
furniture, deterioration of, 1:88
generally, 1:83
holiday letting out of season, 1:84
inherited tenancy, 1:85-86
landlord's works, 1:84-85
mandatory grounds,1:84-86
ministers of religion, 1:84
mortgaged property, 1:84
nuisance, 1:88
rent arrears, 1:86, 1:87
returning home owner, 1:84
specimen form of order, **4:150-151**
student letting, 1:84
suitable alternative accommodation, 1:87
tied accommodation, 1:88
rights of tenants,
generally, 2:5-6
tenants' guarantees, 2:6-7
shorthold. *See* Assured shorthold tenancy
subletting, 2:46
succession,
common law, at, 2:23-24
contractual succession clauses, 2:26-30
generally, 2:23
Housing Act 1988, under, 2:24-25
who is successor, 2:25
who succeeds, 2:25
suitable alternative accommodation,
comparison with local authority practice, 1:94
furniture, 1:94
generally, 1:93
local authority certificate, 1:93
location, 1:95
reluctant tenants, 1:94-95
suitability, 1:93-94
tenancy agreement, 2:54-55

Behaviour of perpetrator
private nuisance and, 3:18
Breach of other term
reasonableness and, 1:102-103
Burden of proof
meaning, **4:154**
Business tenancy
assured tenancy, exclusion from, 1:40
secure tenancy, exclusion from, 1:38

Change of landlord
assured tenancy, 1:42
secure tenancy, 1:42
Charity
secure tenant, grounds for possession against, 1:79
Closing speeches
possession proceedings, **4:81**
Cockroaches
private nuisance, as, 3:17
Cohabitees
rights of, 1:111-112
Commencing possession proceedings. *See* Possession proceedings
Commission for Racial Equality
racial harassment, meaning, 3:70
Committal proceedings
meaning, **4:154**
Committees
representation on, 2:76-77
Common law
meaning, 3:99
public nuisance, 3:23-24
succession at, 2:10, 2:23-24
Common parts
damage to, 1:74
Complaints
neighbours, from, 1:72
nuisance, relating to, 3:39-40

Compulsory competitive tendering
- local authority, by, 2:89
- nuisance and, 3:43-44

Conditions for security of tenure
- abandonment, 1:53-54
- assured tenancy, 1:44
- dwelling-house, 1:44
- gaining possession, 1:55
- generally, 1:43
- let as separate dwelling,
  - meaning, 1:45-46
  - separate, meaning, 1:45
  - shared accomodation, 1:45-46
- lodgers,

Conditions for security of
  - generally, 1:51
  - illegal occupation, 1:52-53
  - loss of security of tenure, 1:51-52
- residence condition, 1:43, 1:46-51
- secure tenancy, 1:43-44
- subletting,
  - generally, 1:51
  - illegal occupation, 1:52-53
  - loss of security of tenure, 1:51-52
- surrender, 1:53-54
- use as home,
  - absence from premises, 1:48-49
  - prolonged absence, 1:48-49
  - residence condition, 1:46-51
  - two homes, 1:49-51

Consent order
- possession proceedings, **4:126-129**

Consolidation
- meaning, **4:154**
- possession proceedings, **4:51-52**

Consultation
- assured tenants, with, 2:75-77
- committees, representation on,
  - generally, 2:77
  - housing associations, 2:78
  - local authorities, 2:77
- housing action trust, declaration of, 2:93
- housing association,
  - sale tenanted to, 2:92
  - sale with vacant possession, 2:93
- local authority, redevelopment by, 2:94
- other forms, 2:77-79
- rent levies for tenants' funds, 2:79
- secure tenants, with,
  - acquisition by new landlord, 2:74-75
  - basic requirement, 2:65
  - generally, 2:65
  - housing action trust, 2:73-74
  - large scale voluntary transfers, 2:71-72
  - managing agents, use of, 2:69-71
  - matters requiring consultation, 2:66-69
  - method of consultation, 2:65-66
  - other duties, 2:69-75
  - outcome of consultation, 2:69
  - redevelopment scheme, declaration of, 2:72-73
- tenants' organisations, funding for, 2:78-79
- *See also* Information

Contractual succession clauses
- alternative approach, 2:29-30
- enforceability of right of assignment, 2:28-29
- generally, 2:26
- housing association, 2:26-27
- local authority, 2:27-28, 2:29

Costs
- possession proceedings. *See* Possession proceedings

Counterclaims
  disrepair, for, 1:100-101
County court
  accelerated procedure in, 1:108, **4:114**
  application to set aside, 1:123-124
  rules, 3:3
  squatters, procedure relating to, 1:113
  suspended order, powers relating to, 1:120-121
  trespassers, procedure relating to, 1:113
Court
  choice of, possession proceedings, **4:13-14**
  commencing possession proceedings, **4:13-14**
  county. *See* County court
Covenants
  meaning, 3:99-100, **4:155**
  right to buy, harassment and, 3:87
Cross-examination
  meaning, **4:155**
  possession proceedings, **4:79-80**
Crown Prosecution Service (CPS)
  criminal proceedings, 3:78
Crown tenancy
  assured tenancy, exclusion from, 1:41

Damage
  private nuisance and, 3:18
Dangerous premises
  private nuisance, as, 3:17
Deceased tenant
  successor, as, 2:19-21
Deception
  tenancy obtained by, 1:75-76
Defences
  possession proceedings. *See* Possession proceedings
  private nuisance, action for,
    generally, 3:21
    ignorance, 3:22
    inevitable accident, 3:21-22
    statutory authorisation, 3:22
Deliberate action
  private nuisance, as, 3:17
Deterioration
  furniture, of, 1:73-75, 1:88
  possession proceedings, **4:39-40**
  premises, of, 1:73-75, 1:88
Development
  home being redeveloped, letter relating to, 1:133-134
  land, 1:32-34, **4:35-36**
  meaning, 1:33
Diary of incidents
  form, 1:143
Directions
  meaning, **4:155**
  possession proceedings. *See* Possession proceedings
Disabled person
  accommodation for, 1:80
Discharge
  suspended possession order, of, 1:122
Disclosure
  exempt information, 2:59
Discovery
  meaning, **4:155**
  possession proceedings. *See* Possession proceedings
Disputes
  management, 2:87-88
Disrepair
  counterclaims for, 1:100-101
  possession proceedings, **4:92-93**
Divorce
  property transfer order, 2:32
Drains
  blocked, as private nuisance, 3:17
Dwelling-house
  deterioration of, 1:73-75, 1:88
  let as separate dwelling,

Dwelling-house – *cont*
let as separate dwelling – *cont*
meaning, 1:45-46
separate, meaning, 1:45
shared accommodation, 1:45-46
meaning, 1:44

Elderly
accommodation for, 1:19-20
Employee
accommodation essential for job, 1:24-25
non-housing property required for, 1:80
rights of, 1:25-28
secure tenancy, exclusion from, 1:32
service occupier, 1:24
service tenant, 1:24
tied accommodation, 1:24
Employment
accommodation related to, 1:76-77, **4:41-42**
Enforcement
assignment, right of, 2:28-29
possession order, of, **4:126**
tenants' guarantee, relating to, 2:6-7
Environmental health officers
nuisance, powers relating to, 3:29, 3:49
possession proceedings, evidence at, **4:72-73**
Environmental Protection Act
statutory nuisance, required action relating to,
individual 'person aggrieved', action by, 3:28-29
local authority, action by, 3:26-28
Estate redevelopment
consultation on declaration of scheme, 2:72-73
generally, 2:91
housing action trust,
declaration of, 2:93-94
housing association,
local authority development,
combination with, 2:95
sale tenanted to, 2:92-93
sale with vacant possession to, 2:93
local authority,
housing association development,
combination with, 2:95
redevelopment by, 2:94-95
Eviction, protection from
abandoned premises, 1:110-111
generally, 1:108
notice to quit, 1:108
period of notice, 1:109
service, 1:110
Evidence
annoyance, of, 1:72
harassment, of, 3:88
hearsay, meaning, **4:156**
in chief, meaning, **4:155**
nuisance, of,
investigation of, 3:41-43
noise nuisance, 3:42-43
private investigator, use of, 3:42
secure tenant, grounds for possession against, 1:72
possession proceedings. *See* Possession proceedings
Ex parte
meaning, 3:100, **4:155**
Exchange
assignment by way of,
consent, grounds for refusing, 2:36-39
generally, 2:35
landlord's written consent, 2:35-36
mutual, 2:35-39
premium, at, 1:76

Exclusive possession
tenant and licensee distinguished, 1:16-17
Exempt landlord
secure tenancy, relating to, 1:41
Expert evidence
possession proceedings, **4:72-74**
Feasibility study
full, 2:85-86
initial, 2:84-85
Fixed term tenancy
forfeiture, 1:62-66
meaning, 2:100, **4:155**
status of tenant, 1:7-8
succession, 2:22
tenancy agreement, 2:54-55
Forfeiture
assured tenancy, of, 1:66
fixed term tenancy, 1:62-66
notice, 1:63-64
provision for, 1:63
re-entry, right of, 1:63
relief from, 1:64-65
rent arrears, action based on, 1:65
secure tenancy, of, 1:65
waiver, 1:64
Forms
possession proceedings, **4:143-153**
Freehold
long leaseholder's right to acquire, 1:6-7
Funding
rent levies for tenants' funds, 2:79
tenants' organisations, for, 2:78-79
Furniture
deterioration of, 1:73-75, 1:88
suitable alternative accommodation, in, 1:94
Further action. *See* Possession proceedings
Further and better particulars
meaning, **4:155-156**
possession proceedings, **4:55-57**

Gaining possession
security of tenure and, 1:55
Grounds for possession. *See* Possession
Handwriting expert
possession proceedings, evidence at, **4:73**
Harassment
aims of guide, 3:5-9
anti-harassment policy, 3:83-84
assistance to victim, 3:88-89
collecting evidence, 3:88
criminal offences, 3:71-74
evidence, 3:88
gang-busting, 3:93
Housing Corporation, duties of, 3:74-75
injunctions, 3:78-80, 3:91-92
laws against,
criminal offences, 3:71-74
generally, 3:69-70
Housing Corporation, duties of, 3:74-75
local authorities, duties and powers of, 3:74-82
racial harassment, nature and extent of, 3:70-71
litigation, 3:89-98
local authorities,
appearing in proceedings brought by others, 3:80
criminal proceedings, 3:78
duties of, 3:74-75
financial assistance, provision of, 3:82
general powers of, 3:76-82
making bye-laws, 3:81-82
obtaining injunctions, 3:78-80
promoting interests of inhabitants, 3:78
section 222 cases, difficulties of, 3:80-81

Harassment – *cont*
  meaning, 3:85, 3:100
  monitoring evidence, 3:88
  obtaining possession, 3:93-98
  practice in case of, 3:83-98
  pre-litigation strategy, 3:89-98
  procedures in case of, 3:83-98
  racial, nature and extent of, 3:70-71
  tenancy agreement,
    generally, 3:84-87
    right to buy covenants, 3:87
  tort of, 3:33-35
  victim, assistance to, 3:88-89
Hearsay evidence
  meaning, **4:156**
  possession proceedings, **4:67-69**
Holiday letting
  exclusion, 1:40
  out of season, 1:84
Home
  matrimonial, 1:111-113
  redevelopment, letter relating to, 1:133-134
  residence condition, 1:46-51
  tenant unable to take care of, 174-75
  two homes, 1:49-51
  use as, 1:46-51
Homeless persons
  accommodation for, 1:34-35, 1:42
Hostel accommodation
  assured shorthold lettings, 1:116
  gaining possession, 1:117-118
  hostel, meaning, 1:117
  Housing Act 1985, 1:114-115
  Housing Act 1988, 1:115-118
  shared living accommodation, 1:115
  tenancy distinguished from licence, 1:17-19, 1:114, 1:115
Housing
  allocation. *See* Allocation of housing
  management. *See* Management
  stock, information on, 2:61
Housing action trust
  consultation duties, 2:73-74
  declaration of,
    consultation, 2:93
    legal status of tenants, 2:94
    possession, grounds for, 2:94
Housing association
  committees, representation on, 2:78
  contractual succession clauses, 2:26-27
  local authority development, combination with, 2:95
  sale tenanted to,
    consultation, 2:92
    legal status of tenants, 2:92
    possession, grounds for, 2:92-93
  sale with vacant possession to,
    consultation, 2:93
    possession, grounds for, 2:93
  secure tenants, functions relating to, 2:4
Housing benefit
  possession action, defence to, **4:93-95**
  rent and, 1:101

Ignorance
  private nuisance action, defence to, 3:22-23
Illegal occupier
  conditions for security of tenure, 1:52-53
  letter to, 1:131-132
Illegal user
  connection between offence and premises, 1:73
  secure tenant, grounds for possession against, 1:73
Immediate order
  possession, for, 1:119, **4:123-124**

Inevitable accident
  private nuisance action,
    defence to, 3:21-22
Informal admission
  meaning, **4:156**
  possession proceedings, **4:69**
Information
  accommodation applications,
    about, 2:58-59
  disclosure, exemption from,
    2:59
  housing allocation, about,
    2:57-58
  landlord authorities,
    meaning, 2:56-57
  provision of, 2:56
  secure tenants, to,
    housing allocations, on,
      2:62
    housing stock, on, 2:61
    management, on, 2:62
    obligations relating to,
      2:60-63
    rents, on, 2:61
    repairs, on, 2:61
    tenancy files, about, 2:58-59
    tenants' guarantee, under,
      2:63-65
  See also Consultation
Inherited tenancy
  possession, grounds for,
    1:85-86
Injunction
  harassment case, in, 3:78-80,
    3:91-92
  meaning, 3:100, **4:156**
  nuisance case, in,
    court, factors taken into
      account by, 3:56-59
    generally, 3:52-53
    interlocutory injunction,
      3:54, 3:55-56
    mandatory injunction, 3:54
    perpetual injunction, 3:54
    prohibitory injunction, 3:54
    quia timet injunction,
      3:54-55
    types of, 3:54-55
Inquiries and investigations
  nuisance, relating to,
    collecting evidence, 3:41-43
    complaints, 3:39-40
    generally, 3:38-39
    giving warnings, 3:39-40
    noise nuisance, 3:42-43
    private investigators, use
      of, 3:42
    substantiated complaints,
      3:39-40
Interlocutory
  meaning, 3:100, **4:156**
Interlocutory injunction
  nuisance case, 3:54, 3:55-56
Interrogatories
  meaning, **4:156**
  possession proceedings,
    4:57-58
Intestacy
  meaning, 2:100
Investigations. *See* Inquiries
  and investigations

Job mobility
  accommodation, 1:35-36
Joint tenants
  notice to quit, 1:128, **4:33-34**
  status of, 1:8-9
  surrender by, 1:126
  termination by, 1:129-130
Judge
  possession proceedings,
    4:76
  reasonableness, discretion
    relating to, 1:96-97

Land
  agricultural, 1:40
  development, 1:32-34, **4:35-36**
  ownership of,
    proof of, **4:22-23**
    tenancy agreement, proof
      of, **4:22-23**
  trespass to, as private
    nuisance, 3:16

Landlord
assignment, written consent to, 2:35-36
change of,
assured tenancy, 1:42
secure tenancy, 1:42
exempt, 1:41
new, acquisition of, 2:74-75
nuisance,
liability for, 3:13-15
responsibility to tackle, 3:12-13
occupier wanted to share or move, 2:49
pick a landlord, 2:74-75
possession proceedings. *See* Possession proceedings
reasonableness, interests relating to, 1:97-98
resident, 1:41
secure tenancy, condition relating to, 1:30-38
superior, 1:9
works of, 1:78-79, 1:84-85, **4:41**
Landlord authorities
meaning, 2:56-57
Large scale voluntary transfers (LSVT)
consultation on, 2:71-72
Leading question
meaning, **4:156**
Lease
extension of, long leaseholder's right to acquire, 1:6-7
long, 1:31-32
Leaseholder. *See* Long leaseholder
Legal aid
possession proceedings, **4:133**
Legal relations
no intention to create, 1:21-24
Letter
annoyance, tenant causing, to, 1:133
home being redeveloped, relating to, 1:133-134
illegal occupier, to, 1:131-132
nuisance, tenant causing, to, 1:133
rent arrears, tenant with, to, 1:132
Licence
elderly, accommodation for, 1:19-20
hostel accommodation, 1:17-19, 1:114, 1:115
residential, 1:10-11
Licensed premises
security of tenure and, 1:37, 1:40
Licensee
meaning, 1:10
occupiers,
landlord, position of, 2:49
wanting to share, 2:48-49
possession proceedings,
generally, **4:114-115**
summary possession, **4:115-119**
residential licence, 1:10-11
service occupier, 1:24
status of, 1:10-11
tenant distinguished from,
accommodation essential for job, 1:24-25
elderly, accommodation for, 1:19-20
employee, rights of, 1:25-28
exceptions, 1:20-28
exclusive possession, 1:16-17
generally, 1:14
hostel accommodation, 1:17-19, 1:114, 1:115
legal relations, no intention to create, 1:21-24
service occupier, 1:24
service tenant, 1:24
tenancy, elements of, 1:14-16
tied accommodation, 1:24
trespasser distinguished from, 1:113

Litigation
  harassment, relating to,
    gang-busting, 3:93
    generally, 3:89-91
    injunctions, 3:91-92
    obtaining possession, 3:93-98
  nuisance, relating to,
    alternatives to, 3:38
    generally, 3:51-52
    injunctions, 3:52-59
    order for possession, 3:59-68
  possession. *See* Possession proceedings
Local authority
  committees, representations on, 2:77
  compulsory competitive tendering, 2:89
  contractual succession clauses, 2:27-28, 2:29
  reasonableness, policy relating to, 1:103-104
  redevelopment by,
    consultation, 2:94
    generally, 2:94
    housing association development, combined with, 2:95
    legal status of tenants, 2:95
    possession, grounds for, 2:95
  secure tenants, functions relating to, 2:4-5
  statutory nuisance, action relating to, 3:26-28
  suitable alternative accommodation, certificate relating to, 1:92, 1:93, 1:94
  tenants' management organisation, support for, 2:83-84
Location
  suitable alternative accommodation, of, 1:95
Lodgers
  assured tenant, taken in by, 2:47
  conditions for security of tenure, 1:51-53
  deterioration caused by, 1:74
  illegal occupation, 1:52-53
  loss of security of tenure, 1:51-52
  secure tenant, taken in by, 2:40-44
London Housing Survey (1993)
  racial harassment, figures on, 3:7
Long leaseholder
  assured tenancy, exclusion of, 1:40
  extension of lease, right to acquire, 1:6-7
  freehold, right to acquire, 1:6-7
  status of, 1:6-7
Loss
  secure tenancy, of, 1:122-123

Management
  balloting,
    further ballot, 2:86-87
    requirements, 2:85
  CCT. *See* Compulsory competitive tendering
  disputes, 2:87-88
  feasibility study,
    full, 2:85-86
    initial, 2:84-85
  proposal notice,
    balloting, 2:85
    right to manage, 2:82-83
    withdrawal, 2:88
  right to manage,
    balloting, 2:85
    compulsory competitive tendering, relationship with, 2:89
    disputes, 2:87-88
    full feasibility study, 2:85-86
    generally, 2:80-81
    initial feasibility study, 2:84-85
    local authority support, 2:83-84

Management – *cont*
  right to manage – *cont*
    notification and further ballot, 2:86-87
    proposal notice, 2:82-83
    registration of organisation, 2:89
    rights acquired, 2:88
    tenants' management organisations, 2:81-82
    withdrawal of notice, 2:88
  secure tenants, information to, 2:62-63
  tenants' organisations,
    disputes, 2:87-88
    funding for, 2:78-79
    local authority support, 2:83-84
    registration, 2:89
    rent levies for tenants' funds, 2:79
    right to manage, 2:81-82
Managing agents
  consultation on use of, 2:69-71
  secure tenancy, 1:31
Mandatory injunction
  nuisance case, 3:54
Matrimonial home
  cohabitees, 1:111-112
  remaining spouse, rights of, 1:112-113
  right to remain in, 1:112
  spouses, 1:112-113
Matrimonial property order
  secure tenancy, relating to, 2:11
Mediation
  meaning, 3:100
  nuisance, relating to,
    generally, 3:45-46
    process, 3:46-48
Medical evidence
  possession proceedings, **4:73-74**
Members of family
  succession, 2:13-15
Mesne tenant
  status of, 1:9-10
Ministers of religion
  possession, grounds for, 1:84
Money judgment
  order including, **4:126**
  proof of, **4:31-32**
  unauthorised occupier, action against, **4:103-105**
Mortgaged property
  assured tenant, grounds for possession against, 1:84

Negligence
  nuisance and, 3:29-31
Neighbourhood
  nature of, private nuisance and, 3:18
Neighbours
  complaints from, 1:72
New tenancy
  assured shorthold, 1:107
Noise nuisance
  evidence of, 3:42-43
  private nuisance, as, 3:16
Non-housing property
  employee, required for, 1:80
Notice
  forfeiture, of, 1:63-64
  section 48, 1:68-69
  seeking possession,
    assured tenancy, 1:61-62, 1:138-142
    commencing possession proceedings, **4:10-13**
    examples, 1:59-60
    generally, 1:58-59
    length of, **4:13**
    meaning, **4:156**
    secure tenancy, 1:60-61, 1:134-138
Notice to quit
  abandoned premises, 1:110-111
  form, 1:142-143
  generally, 1:108
  hostel accommodation, 1:117-118

Notice to quit – *cont*
joint tenants, by, 1:128, **4:33-34**
meaning, **4:157**
period of notice, 1:109
service, 1:110
tenant, by,
contents, 1:128
effect, 1:129
generally, 1:128
joint tenants, 1:128
Nuisance
agencies used to deal with,
environmental health officers, 3:49
planning departments, 3:49-50
police, 3:50
RSPCA, 3:50
social services, 3:49
aims of guide, 3:5-9
annoyance and, 3:61-63
assured tenant, grounds for possession against, 1:88
causes of, 3:2-5
compulsory competitive tendering of housing management, 3:43-44
consequences of, 3:2-5
definitions, 3:10-11
evidence, 1:72, 3:41-43
inquiries and investigations,
collecting evidence, 3:41-43
complaints, 3:39-40
generally, 3:38-39
giving warnings, 3:39-40
noise nuisance, 3:42-43
private investigator, use of, 3:42
substantiated complaints, 3:39-40
invalid excuses for, 3:23
laws against,
definitions, 3:10-11
generally, 3:10
negligence and nuisance, 3:29-31
private nuisance, 3:15-23
public nuisance, 3:23-24
rule in *Rylands v Fletcher*, 3:31-33
social landlords' responsibility and liability, 3:12-15
statutory nuisance, 3:24-29
letter to tenant causing, 1:133
liability for, 3:13-15
litigation,
alternatives to, 3:38
generally, 3:51-52
injunctions, 3:52-59
order for possession, 3:59-68
meaning, 3:100, **4:157**
mediation,
generally, 3:45-46
process, 3:46-48
negligence and, 3:29-31
neighbours, complaints from, 1:72
noise,
evidence of, 3:42-43
private nuisance, as, 3:16
possession proceedings,
generally, **4:106-109**
proof of nuisance, **4:39**
return date, **4:110**
undertakings, **4:110-112**
witness statement, **4:110**
private,
assessing unreasonable use, 3:17-19
defences, 3:21-23
generally, 3:15-16
invalid excuses for, 3:23
types of, 3:16-17
who can be sued, 3:20
who can sue, 3:19-20
probationary tenancies, 3:44-45
public, 3:23-24
reasonableness in case of, 1:98-99, 3:64-68
responsibility to tackle, 3:12-13

Nuisance – *cont*
rule in *Rylands v Fletcher,*
complainant, matters to be proved by, 3:31-33
generally, 3:31
secure tenant, grounds for possession against, 1:70-73
social landlord,
liability of, 3:13-15
responsibility and liability, 3:12-15
responsibility to tackle nuisance, 3:12-13
statutory,
Environmental Protection Act, required action under, 3:26-29
generally, 3:24-25
nuisance, meaning, 3:26
prejudicial to health, 3:25-26
those who live with tenant, caused by, 1:71
visitors, caused by, 1:71
who can be sued, 3:20, 3:36-37
who can sue, 3:19-20, 3:36-37

Oath
evidence on, **4:77**
Occupation
illegal, 1:52-53, 1:131-132
owner occupier. *See* Owner occupier
sharing,
landlord wanting occupier to share, 2:49
occupier wanting to share, 2:48-49
status of occupier,
examples, 1:12-13
generally, 1:5
licensee, 1:10-11
owner occupier, 1:5-7
tenant, 1:7-10
trespasser, 1:11
unauthorised occupier, meaning, **4:158**
Orders
possession. *See* Possession orders
unless, meaning, **4:158**
Outright order
possession, for, 1:120, **4:124-125**
Overcrowding
secure tenant, grounds for possession against, 1:78
Owner
land, of,
proof of, **4:22-23**
tenancy agreement, proof of, **4:22-23**
returning home, 1:84
Owner occupier
long leaseholder,
extension of lease, right to acquire, 1:6-7
freehold, right to acquire, 1:6-7
status of, 1:6-7
meaning, 1:5-6
status of, 1:5-7

Participation
committees, representation on,
generally, 2:77
housing authorities, 2:78
local authorities, 2:77
rent levies for tenants' funds, 2:79
tenants' organisations, funding for, 2:78-79
See also Consultation
Particulars of claim
meaning, **4:157**
possession proceedings. *See* Possession proceedings
Parties
possession proceedings, **4:20, 4:138-140**
Period of notice
eviction, protection from, 1:109

Periodic tenancy
meaning, 2:100, **4:157**
status of tenant, 1:7-8
statutory, 2:46
tenancy agreement, 2:54-55
Perpetual injunction
nuisance case, 3:54
Personal files
access to, 2:58-59
Pets
secure tenant, grounds for possession against, 1:70
Plaintiff
meaning, **4:157**
Planning departments
nuisance, dealing with problems of, 3:49-50
Pleadings
meaning, **4:157**
possession proceedings, **4:14-20, 4:55-58**
Police
nuisance, dealing with problems of, 3:50
Possession
assured shorthold tenancy, 1:107, **4:113-114**
assured tenant, grounds for possession against,
annoyance, 1:88
breach of term of tenancy, 1:87
deterioration of dwelling-house, 1:88
discretionary grounds, 1:86-88
furniture, deterioration of, 1:88
generally, 1:83
holiday letting out of season, 1:84
inherited tenancy, 1:85-86
landlord's works, 1:84-85
mandatory grounds, 1:84-86
ministers of religion, 1:84
mortgaged property, 1:84
nuisance, 1:88
rent arrears, 1:86, 1:87
returning home owner, 1:84
specimen form of order, **4:150-151**
student letting, 1:84
suitable alternative accommodation, 1:87
tied accommodation, 1:88
avoiding formal proceedings, 1:57-58
exclusive, 1:16-17
gaining, 1:55
harassment case, in, 3:93-98
hostel accommodation, of, 1:117-118
housing action trust, declaration of, 2:94
housing association,
sale tenanted to, 2:92-93
sale with vacant possession, 2:93
local authority, redevelopment by, 2:95
notice seeking,
assured tenancy, 1:61-62, 1:138-142
commencing possession proceedings, **4:10-13**
generally, 1:58-60
length of, **4:13**
meaning, **4:156**
rent arrears, effect on, 1:99-100
secure tenancy, 1:60-61, 1:134-138
nuisance case, order in,
annoyance, nuisance and, 3:61-63
generally, 3:59-60
grounds for possession, 3:60-64
procedure, 3:60
reasonableness in granting possession, 3:64-68
tenancy agreement, breach of, 3:60-61
waste, 3:63-64

Possession – *cont*
orders. *See* Possession orders
proceedings. *See* Possession proceedings
reasonableness. *See* Reasonableness
rent arrears,
discretionary grounds, 1:87
mandatory grounds, 1:86
proceedings. *See* Possession proceedings
secure tenant, grounds for possession against,
accommodation pending works, 1:77-78
annoyance, 1:70-73
breach of other term, 1:70
charitable purposes, 1:79
deception, tenancy obtained by, 1:75-76
deterioration of premises, 1:73-75
disabled, accommodation for, 1:80
employment related accommodation, 1:76-77
exchange at premium, 1:76
furniture, deterioration of, 1:73-75
grounds 1-8, 1:67-78
grounds 9-11, 1:78-79
grounds 12-16, 1:79-82
landlord's works, 1:78-79
non-housing property required for employee, 1:80
nuisance, 1:70-73
overcrowding, 1:78
rent arrears, 1:67-69
sheltered accommodation, 1:81
special needs accommodation, 1:80-81
under-occupation, 1:81-82
seeking,
avoiding formal proceedings, 1:57-58
fixed term tenancy, 1:62-66
forfeiture, 1:62-66
grounds for, 1:56-57
procedure, 1:58-62
security provided, 1:56
successor,
assignee, seeking possession against, 2:34-35
under-occupation by, 2:22
suitable alternative accommodation. *See* Suitable alternative accommodation
under-occupation by successor, for, 2:22
warrant for, 1:122, **4:134-135**
Possession orders
acceptance of rent, 1:123
application to set aside, 1:123-124
assured tenancies, **4:150-151**
consent order, **4:126-129**
costs,
generally, **4:129-130**
interlocutory matters, in, **4:130-132**
return date, orders at, **4:132**
types of order, **4:130-132**
enforcement of, **4:126**
generally, 1:119, **4:123**
immediate, 1:119, **4:123-124**
leave, not to be enforced without, **4:126**
legal aid, **4:133**
loss of secure tenancy, 1:122-123
money judgment, **4:126**
nuisance case, 3:59-68
outright, 1:120, **4:124-125**
rent arrears cases,
arrears at significant level, **4:90-91**

Possession orders – *cont*
rent arrears cases – *cont*
arrears cleared, **4:89**
arrears substantially cleared and agreement about remainder, **4:89-90**
options for orders, **4:88-92**
very significant arrears, **4:91-92**
rented property, **4:152-153**
setting aside, **4:137-138**
specimen form,
assured tenancy, **4:150-151**
possession suspended, **4:152-153**
summary possession, **4:119**
suspended, 1:101, 1:120-122, **4:125, 4:152-153**
warrant for possession, 1:122
Possession proceedings
accelerated procedure, 1:108, **4:114**
accommodation,
employees, required for, **4:41-42**
pending works, **4:40-41**
adjournment,
court's attitude to request, **4:50**
defence raised, **4:50-51**
generally, **4:48**
inability to prove case, **4:48-49**
return date, change of circumstances before, **4:49-50**
affidavit,
evidence, **4:71-72**
meaning, **4:154**
summary possession, **4:116**
annoyance, based on,
generally, **4:106-109**
proof of, **4:39**
return date, **4:110**
undertakings, **4:110-112**
witness statement, **4:110**
appeal, **4:136-137**
assured shorthold tenants,
accelerated possession procedure, **4:114**
generally, **4:113-114**
burden of proof, **4:65-66, 4:154**
calculation of court time, **4:64**
checklists,
death of tenant, **4:33**
generally, **4:32**
loss of security of tenure, **4:32-33**
notice to quit by joint tenant, **4:33-34**
security of tenure, exceptions to, **4:34-37**
statutory grounds for possession, claims based on, **4:37-43**
choice of court, **4:13-14**
closing speeches, **4:81**
commencing,
choice of court, **4:13-14**
generally, **4:7**
parties, **4:20**
pleadings, **4:14-20**
steps before action, **4:7-8**
summons, **4:14-20**
termination of tenancy agreement, **4:8-13**
consent order, **4:126-129**
consolidation, **4:51-52, 4:51-52**
costs,
generally, **4:129-130**
interlocutory matters, in, **4:130-132**
return date, orders at, **4:132**
types of order, **4:130-132**
County Court Rules, **4:3**
cross-examination, **4:79-80, 4:155**
death of tenant, **4:33**
defence,
case, **4:80-81**
disrepair as, **4:92-93**
housing benefit as, **4:93-95**

Possession proceedings – *cont*
defence – *cont*
Landlord and Tenant Act 1987, under, **4:95**
rent arrears cases, **4:92-95**
return date, raised at, **4:45-46, 4:50-51**
unauthorised occupier, action against, **4:98-103**
deterioration of premises, **4:39-40**
development land, **4:35-36**
directions,
calculation of court time, **4:64**
generally, **4:54-55**
meaning, **4:155**
typical, **4:63-64**
discovery,
exceptions, **4:60**
filing, **4:58-59**
lists, by, **4:59**
meaning, **4:155**
pretrial procedure, **4:58-60**
disrepair as defence, **4:92-93**
employees, accommodation required for, **4:41-42**
environmental health officer, evidence of, **4:72-73**
evidence,
affidavit, **4:71-72, 4:154**
burden of proof, **4:65-66, 4:154**
Civil Evidence Act, under, **4:70-71**
evidence-in-chief, **4:78-79, 4:155**
expert, **4:72-74**
generally, **4:65**
giving, **4:77**
hearsay, **4:67-69, 4:156**
informal admission, **4:69, 4:156**
medical, **4:73-74**
oath, on, **4:77**
public documents, **4:69-70**
rent arrears cases, **4:87-88**
types of, **4:66-74**
unauthorised occupier, action against, **4:97-98**
expert evidence,
environmental health officers, **4:72-73**
generally, **4:72**
handwriting experts, **4:73**
medical evidence, **4:73-74**
surveyors, **4:73**
forms, **4:143-153**
further action,
appeal, **4:136-137**
generally, **4:134**
setting aside order, **4:137-138**
stay of execution, **4:137**
subsequent conduct by parties, **4:138-140**
warrant for possession, **4:134-135**
further and better particulars,
meaning, **4:155-156**
pretrial procedure, **4:55-57**
handwriting expert, evidence of, **4:73**
hearsay evidence, **4:67-69, 4:156**
housing benefit as defence, **4:93-95**
informal admission, **4:69, 4:156**
interrogatories,
meaning, **4:156**
pretrial procedure, **4:57-58**
judges, **4:76**
Landlord and Tenant Act 1987, defence under, **4:95**
landlord's case,
cross-examination, **4:79-80**
evidence-in-chief, **4:78-79**
re-examination, **4:80**
legal aid, **4:133**
licensees,
generally, **4:114-115**
summary possession, **4:115-119**

Possession proceedings – *cont*
limited security,
assured shorthold, **4:113-114**
licensees, **4:114-119**
medical evidence, **4:73-74**
money judgment,
order including, **4:126**
proof of, **4:31-32**
unauthorised occupier, action against, **4:103-105**
notice to quit,
joint tenant, by, **4:33-34**
meaning, **4:157**
nuisance, based on,
generally, **4:106-109**
proof of, **4:39**
return date, **4:110**
undertakings, **4:110-112**
witness statement, **4:110**
oath, evidence on, **4:77**
opening, **4:77**
orders. *See* Possession orders
ownership of land,
proof of, **4:22-23**
tenancy agreement, proof of, **4:22-23**
particulars of claim,
content of, **4:17-20**
meaning, **4:157**
rent arrears cases, **4:18-20**, **4:144-147**
specimen form, **4:144-147**
parties,
commencing proceedings, **4:20**
subsequent conduct by, **4:138-140**
pleadings,
commencing proceedings, **4:14-20**
meaning, **4:157**
pretrial procedure, **4:55-58**
pretrial procedure,
directions, **4:54-55**, **4:63-64**
generally, **4:53-54**
procedural steps, **4:55-62**
unless orders, **4:62-63**
proof,
burden of, **4:65-66**, **4:154**
checklists, **4:32-43**
inability to prove case, **4:48-49**
money judgments, **4:31-32**
ownership of land, **4:22-23**
reason for seeking possession, **4:26-31**
return date, **4:47-52**
tenant's interest, termination of, **4:23-25**
unauthorised occupier, action against, **4:98**
what needs to be proved, **4:21-43**
re-examination, **4:80**, **4:157**
reason for seeking possession,
landlord's circumstances, **4:27-28**
non-secure/assured tenants, **4:26**
reasonableness, **4:26-28**
secure/assured tenants, **4:26**
suitable alternative accommodation, **4:28-31**
tenant's circumstances, **4:27**
rent arrears cases,
arrears at significant level, **4:90-91**
arrears cleared, **4:89**
arrears substantially cleared and agreement about remainder, **4:89-90**
defences, **4:92-95**
disrepair as defence, **4:92-93**
evidence of arrears, **4:88**
generally, **4:85**
housing benefit as defence, **4:93-94**
Landlord and Tenant Act 1987, defence under, **4:95**
orders, options for, **4:88-92**

Possession proceedings – *cont*
rent arrears cases – *cont*
particulars of claim, **4:18-20, 4:144-147**
required evidence, **4:87-88**
statutory grounds for possession, **4:37-39, 4:85-87**
very significant arrears, **4:91-92**
return date,
adjournments, **4:48-51**
annoyance, action based on, **4:110**
change of circumstances before, **4:49-50**
consolidation, **4:51-52**
costs orders at, **4:132**
defences raised at, **4:45-46, 4:50-51**
generally, **4:44**
inability to prove case, **4:48-49**
meaning, **4:157**
nature of hearing, **4:44-47**
nuisance, action based on, **4:110**
proving case, **4:47-52**
typical outcomes at, **4:46-47**
unauthorised occupier, action against, **4:105-106**
security of tenure,
exceptions to, **4:34-37**
loss of, **4:32-33**
service,
summary possession, **4:117-118**
tenant's interest, termination of, **4:23-25**
setting aside order, **4:137-138**
settlement, **4:76**
short-life user property, **4:35-36**
specimen forms, **4:143-153**
statutory grounds for possession, claims based on,
accommodation pending works, **4:40-41**
annoyance to neighbours, **4:39**
deterioration of premises, **4:39-40**
employees, accommodation required for, **4:41-42**
landlord's works, **4:41**
nuisance to neighbours, **4:39**
rent arrears, **4:37-39**
under-occupation, **4:42-43**
stay of execution, **4:137**
subleasing schemes, **4:36-37**
suitable alternative accommodation,
landlords who are not local authorities, **4:30-31**
local authority tenants, **4:29-30**
proof of, **4:28-31**
summary possession,
affidavit, **4:116**
hearing, **4:118-119**
named respondent, service on, **4:117**
order, **4:119**
procedure, **4:115**
unknown persons, service on, **4:117-118**
summons,
commencing proceedings, **4:14-20**
content of, **4:17**
meaning, **4:158**
specimen form, **4:143**
surveyor, evidence of, **4:73**
tenant's interest, termination of,
deceased tenants, **4:25**
form of notice, **4:23**
physically serving notice, **4:24-25**
proof of, **4:23-25**
service of notice, **4:23-25**
termination of tenancy agreement,

Possession proceedings – *cont*
termination of tenancy
agreement – *cont*
generally, **4:8-9**
length of notice, **4:13**
notice seeking
possession, **4:10-13**
tied accommodation, **4:34-35**
trial,
closing speeches, **4:81**
cross-examination, **4:79-80**
defence case, **4:80-81**
evidence-in-chief, **4:78-79**
giving evidence, **4:77**
judges, **4:76**
landlord's case, **4:78-80**
oath, evidence on, **4:77**
opening, **4:77**
outline, **4:75-76**
re-examination, **4:80**
settlement, **4:76**
typical directions, **4:63-64**
unauthorised occupier,
defences, **4:98-100**
generally, **4:96-97**
meaning, **4:96**, **4:158**
money judgment,
4:103-105
new tenancy, creation of,
4:100-103
proof in court, **4:98**
required evidence, **4:97-98**
return date, **4:105-106**
spouses, rights of, **4:98**
temporarily absent tenant,
4:98-100
under-occupation, **4:42-43**
undertaking,
annoyance, action based
on, **4:110-112**
meaning, **4:158**
nuisance, action based on,
4:110-112
specimen form, **4:148-149**
unless order,
meaning, **4:158**
pretrial procedure, **4:62-63**
warrant for possession,
4:134-135
witness statements,
annoyance, action based
on, **4:110**
meaning, **4:158**
nuisance, action based on,
4:110
pretrial procedure, **4:60-62**
works,
accommodation pending,
4:40-41
landlord, of, **4:41**
Premium
exchange at, 1:76
Pretrial procedure. *See*
Possession proceedings
Principal home
secure tenancy, 2:12-13
Private investigator
nuisance, investigation of,
3:42
Private nuisance
assessing unreasonable use,
behaviour of perpetrator,
3:18
damage, 3:18
generally, 3:17-18
neighbourhood, nature of,
3:18
generally, 3:15-16
invalid excuses for, 3:23
types of, 3:16-17
who can be sued, 3:20
who can sue, 3:19-20
Probationary tenancy
nuisance, solution to problem
of, 3:44-45
Prohibitory injunction
nuisance case, 3:54
Proof
assignment, of, 2:33-34
burden of, meaning, **4:154**
possession proceedings. *See*
Possession proceedings
Property transfer order
assignment pursuant to, 2:32

Protection from eviction. *See* Eviction, protection from
Public nuisance
  common law, at, 3:23-24
  criminal offence, as, 3:23

Quia timet injunction
  nuisance case, 3:54-55
Quiet enjoyment
  meaning, 3:100-101, **4:157**

Racial harassment
  extent of, 3:70-71
  London Housing Survey (1993) figures on, 3:7
  nature of, 3:70-71
  See also Harassment
Rateable values
  high, tenancy of premises with, 1:39
Re-examination
  meaning, **4:157**
  possession proceedings, **4:80**
Reason for seeking possession. *See* Possession proceedings
Reasonableness
  breach of other term, 1:102-103
  circumstances to be considered, 1:97-99
  council policy, 1:103-104
  generally, 1:96
  granting possession, 3:64-68
  judge's discretion, 1:96-97
  landlord, interests of, 1:97-98
  nuisance cases, 1:98-99, 3:64-68
  possession, reason for seeking, **4:26-28**
  private nuisance,
    assessing unreasonable use, 3:17-19
    behaviour of perpetrator, 3:18
    damage, 3:18
    neighbourhood, nature of, 3:18
  remedying breach, 1:102-103
  rent arrears,
    amount, 1:99
    disrepair, counterclaims for, 1:100-101
    example, 1:101-102
    generally, 1:99
    housing benefit, rent and, 1:101
    notice seeking possession, effect of, 1:99-100
    reasons for arrears, 1:100
    suspended orders, 1:101
  tenant, interests of, 1:97
Redevelopment. *See* Estate redevelopment
Registration
  tenants' management organisation, of, 2:89
Remedy
  breach of other term, 1:102-103
Rent arrears
  earlier, 1:68
  forfeiture action based on, 1:65
  letter to tenant with, 1:132
  possession,
    discretionary grounds, 1:87
    mandatory grounds, 1:86
    proceedings. *See* Possession proceedings
  reasonableness relating to,
    amount, 1:99
    counterclaims for disrepair, 1:100-101
    example, 1:101-102
    generally, 1:99
    housing benefit, rent and, 1:101
    notice seeking possession, effect of, 1:99-100
    reasons for arrears, 1:100
    suspended orders, 1:101
  reasons for, 1:100
  section 48 notice, 1:68-69
  secure tenant, grounds for possession against, 1:67-69

Rents
arrears. *See* Rent arrears
secure tenants, information to, 2:61
tenants' funds, rent levies for, 2:79
Repairs
secure tenants, information to, 2:61
Residence condition
security of tenure, 1:43, 1:46-51
succession, 2:15-19
Resident landlord
assured tenancy, exemption from, 1:41
Residential licence
meaning, 1:10-11
Return date
meaning, **4:157**
possession proceedings. *See* Possession proceedings
Returning home owner
possession, mandatory grounds for, 1:84
Right to buy covenants
harassment, prevention of, 3:87
Right to manage. *See* Management
Rights of tenants
ancillary, summary of, 2:3-4
assignment. *See* Assignment
assured tenant,
generally, 2:5-6
tenants' guarantees, 2:6-7
consultation. *See* Consultation
historical background,
ancillary rights, summary of, 2:3-4
assured tenant, 2:5-7
generally, 2:1
secure tenant, subsequent changes for, 2:4-5
Tenants' Charter 1980, 2:2-4
information. *See* Information
management. *See* Management
participation. *See* Participation
succession. *See* Succession
Royal Society for Prevention of Cruelty to Animals (RSPCA)
nuisance, dealing with problems of, 3:50
Rylands v Fletcher, rule in nuisance and, 3:31-33

Section 48 notice
secure tenant, grounds for possession against, 1:68-69
Secure tenancy
assignment of,
exchange, by way of, 2:35-39
generally, 2:32
mutual exchange, 2:35-39
potential successor, to, 2:32-33
proof of assignment, 2:33-34
property transfer order, 2:32
successor assignee, seeking possession against, 2:34-35
change of landlord, 1:42
conditions, 1:43-44
consultation with secure tenants,
acquisition by new landlord, 2:74-75
basic requirement, 2:65
generally, 2:65
housing action trusts, 2:73-74
large scale voluntary transfers, 2:71-72
managing agents, use of, 2:69-71
matters requiring consultation, 2:66-69
method of consultation, 2:65-66
other duties, 2:69-75

Secure tenancy – *cont*
consultation with secure tenants – *cont*
outcome of consultation, 2:69
redevelopment scheme, declaration of, 2:72-73
exceptions,
accommodation pending works, 1:37
agricultural holdings, 1:37
almshouses, 1:38
business lettings, 1:38
development land, 1:32-34
employee accommodation, 1:32
generally, 1:31
homeless persons, accommodation for, 1:34-35
job mobility accommodation, 1:35-36
licensed premises, 1:37
long lease, 1:31-32
student lettings, 1:37-38
subleasing scheme, 1:36-37
forfeiture of, 1:65
generally, 1:29
housing association, functions of, 2:4
information to secure tenants,
housing allocations, on, 2:62
housing stock, on, 2:61
management, on, 2:62
obligations, 2:60-63
rents, on, 2:61
repairs, 2:61
landlord,
change of, 1:42
condition, 1:30-38
local authority, functions of, 2:4-5
lodgers, 2:40-44
loss of, 1:122-123
managing agents, 1:31
meaning, 2:100, 3:101, **4:158**
notice seeking possession of, 1:60-61, 1:134-138
possession, grounds for,
accommodation pending works, 1:77-78
annoyance, 1:70-73
breach of other term, 1:70
charitable purposes, 1:79
deception, tenancy obtained by, 1:75-76
deterioration of premises, 1:73-75
disabled, accommodation for, 1:80
employment related accommodation, 1:76-77
exchange at premium, 1:76
furniture, deterioration of, 1:73-75
grounds 1-8, 1:67-68
grounds 9-11, 1:78-79
grounds 12-16, 1:79-82
landlord's works, 1:78-79
non-housing property required for employee, 1:80
nuisance, 1:70-73
overcrowding, 1:78
pets, 1:70
rent arrears, 1:67-69
sheltered accommodation, 1:81
special needs accommodation, 1:80-81
under-occupation, 1:81-82
waiver of breach, 1:70
spouse of tenant, 2:13
subletting, 2:39-40
succession,
common law, succession at, 2:10
deceased tenant already successor, 2:19-21
fixed term tenancy, 2:22
generally, 2:10
Housing Act 1985, under, 2:11-21, 2:97

Secure tenancy – *cont*
succession – *cont*
matrimonial property order, 2:11
only or principal home, 2:12-13
other members of family, 2:13-15
residence condition, 2:15-19
spouse of tenant, 2:13
succession to whom, 2:21
termination, 2:10-11
under-occupation by successor, possession for, 2:22
who may succeed, 2:11-12
suitable alternative accommodation,
allocation policy, 1:91-92
generally, 1:89-90
local authority certificate, 1:92
needs of tenant, 1:90-91
tenancy agreement, 2:50-54
to whom, 2:21
under-occupation by successor, possession for, 2:22
who may succeed, 2:11-12, 2:25
Security of tenure
conditions. *See* Conditions for security of tenure
lodgers, 2:47-48
main purpose of book, 1:2-3
meaning, 1:1
possession proceedings. *See* Possession proceedings
subtenants, 2:47-48
summary of legislation, 1:1-2
Seeking possession
avoiding formal proceedings, 1:57-58
fixed term tenancy, 1:62-66
forfeiture, 1:62-66
grounds for, 1:56-57
procedure, 1:58-62
security provided, 1:56
Separation
property transfer order, 2:32
Service
notice to quit, of, 1:110
Service occupier
meaning, 1:24
Service tenant
meaning, 1:24
Setting aside
possession order, **4:137-138**
Settlement
possession proceedings, **4:76**
Shared accommodation
security of tenure, conditions for, 1:45-46
Sheltered accommodation
secure tenant, grounds for possession against, 1:81
Smells
private nuisance, as, 3:16
Social services
nuisance, dealing with problems of, 3:49
Special needs accommodation
secure tenant, grounds for possession against, 1:80-81
Spouses
matrimonial home, rights relating to, 1:112-113
succession, requirements for, 2:13
suspended order, powers relating to, 1:121
Squatters
nature of, 1:113
status of, 1:11
State of affairs
private nuisance, as, 3:17
Status of occupier
examples, 1:12-13
generally, 1:5
housing action trust, declaration of, 2:94
housing association, sale tenanted to, 2:92

Status of occupier – *cont*
licensee,
generally, 1:10
residential licence, 1:10-11
local authority,
redevelopment by, 2:95
owner occupier,
long leaseholder, 1:6-7
owner, meaning, 1:5-6
tenant,
assignment of tenancy, 1:8
fixed term, 1:7-8
generally, 1:7
joint tenants, 1:8-9
periodic tenancy, 1:7-8
subtenants, 1:9-10
succession to tenancy, 1:8
transfer of tenancy, 1:8
written agreement, 1:8
trespasser, 1:11
Statutory authorisation
private nuisance action, defence to, 3:22
Statutory grounds for possession. *See* Possession proceedings
Statutory nuisance
Environmental Protection Act, required action under,
individual 'person aggrieved', action by, 3:28-29
local authority, action by, 3:26-28
generally, 3:24-25
nuisance, meaning, 3:26
prejudicial to health, 3:25-26
Statutory periodic tenancy
assignment, 2:46
Stay of execution
possession proceedings, **4:137**
Steps before action
possession proceedings, **4:7-8**
Student lettings
assured tenancy, exclusion from, 1:40
possession, grounds for, 1:84
secure tenancy, exclusion from, 1:37-38
Subleasing scheme
possession proceedings, **4:36-37**
secure tenancy, 1:36-37
Subletting
assured tenancy, 2:46
conditions for security of tenure, 1:51-53
illegal occupation, 1:52-53
loss of security of tenure, 1:51-52
secure tenancy, 2:39-40
Subtenants
deterioration caused by, 1:74
lodgers distinguished from, 2:41-44
security of, 2:47-48
status of, 1:9-10
Succession
assured tenancy,
common law, succession at, 2:23-24
contractual succession clauses, 2:26-30
generally, 2:23
Housing Act 1988, succession under, 2:24-25
who is successor, 2:25
who succeeds, 2:25
common law, at, 2:10, 2:23-24
contractual clauses,
alternative approach, 2:29-30
enforceability of right of assignment, 2:28-29
generally, 2:26
housing association, 2:26-27
local authority, 2:27-28, 2:29
deceased tenant already successor, 2:19-21
effects of, 2:9-10
generally, 2:8-9

Succession – *cont*
meaning, 1:8
members of family, 2:13-15
only or principal home, 2:12-13
potential successor, assignment to, 2:32-33
residence condition, 2:15-19
secure tenancy,
common law, succession at, 2:10
deceased tenant already successor, 2:19-21
fixed term tenancy, 2:22
generally, 2:10
Housing Act 1985, succession under, 2:11-21, 2:97
matrimonial property order, 2:11
only or principal home, 2:12-13
other members of family, 2:13-15
residence condition, 2:15-19
spouse of tenant, 2:13
succession to whom, 2:21
termination, 2:10-11
under-occupation by successor, possession for, 2:22
who may succeed, 2:11-12
spouse of tenant, 2:13
successor assignee, seeking possession against, 2:34-35
to whom, 2:21
under-occupation by successor, possession for, 2:22
who may succeed, 2:11-12, 2:25
Suitable alternative accommodation
assured tenant,
comparison with local authority practice, 1:94
furniture, 1:94
generally, 1:93
local authority certificate, 1:93
location, 1:95
reluctant tenants, 1:94-95
suitability, 1:93-94
generally, 1:89
possession proceedings, **4:28-31**
possession, discretionary grounds for, 1:87
secure tenant,
allocation policy, 1:91-92
generally, 1:89-90
local authority certificate, 1:92
needs of, 1:90-91
Summary possession. *See* Possession proceedings
Summons
commencing possession proceedings, **4:14-20**
meaning, **4:158**
possession proceedings,
commencing proceedings, **4:14-20**
content, **4:17**
specimen form, **4:143**
Surrender
agreement to surrender, 1:125
conditions for security of tenure, 1:53-54
examples, 1:126-128
joint tenants, by, 1:126
nature of, 1:125
operation of law, by, 1:126
Surveyor
possession proceedings, evidence at, **4:73**
Suspended order
court, powers of, 1:120-121
discharge, 1:122
nature of, 1:120
possession, for, 1:101, 1:120-122, **4:125**, **4:152-153**
rent arrears case, 1:101
spouses, 1:121
terms, 1:121
varying terms, 1:121

Tenancy
agreement,
assured tenancy, 2:54-55
breach of, as ground for possession, 3:60-61
changing terms of, 2:50-55
covenant, meaning, 2:99
fixed term tenancy, 2:54
harassment, prevention of, 3:84-87
periodic tenancy, 2:54-55
secure tenancy, 2:50-54
termination of, **4:8-13**
assignment of. *See* Assignment
assured. *See* Assured tenancy
change of landlord, 1:42
Crown, 1:41
deception, obtained by, 1:75-76
elements of, 1:14-16
exceptions, 1:20-28
files, information about, 2:58-59
fixed term. *See* Fixed term tenancy
inherited, 1:85-86
landlord,
change of, 1:42
condition, 1:30-38
legal relations, no intention to create, 1:21-24
periodic. *See* Periodic tenancy
probationary, 3:44-45
rights of tenants. *See* Rights of tenants
secure. *See* Secure tenancy
Street v Mountford, 1:15-16
succession to. *See* Succession
surrender of, 1:53-54
transfer of, 1:8
Tenant satisfaction survey
nuisance, causes of, 3:4
Tenants
assignment of tenancy, 1:8
fixed term tenancy, 1:7-8
joint. *See* Joint tenants
licensee distinguished from,
accommodation essential for job, 1:24-25
elderly, accommodation for, 1:19-20
employee, rights of, 1:25-28
exceptions, 1:20-28
exclusive possession, 1:16-17
generally, 1:14
hostel accommodation, 1:17-19, 1:114, 1:115
legal relations, no intention to create, 1:21-24
service occupier, 1:24
service tenant, 1:24
tenancy, elements of, 1:14-16
tied accommodation, 1:24
mesne, 1:9-10
periodic tenancy, 1:7-8
possession proceedings. *See* Possession proceedings
reasonableness, interests relating to, 1:97
rights. *See* Rights of tenants
service, 1:24
status of, 1:7-10
subtenants, 1:9-10
succession to tenancy, 1:8
termination by,
generally, 1:125
joint tenants, 1:126, 1:129-130
notice to quit, 1:128-129
surrender, 1:125-128
transfer of tenancy, 1:8
unable to take care of home, 1:74-75
written agreement, 1:8
Tenants' guarantee
enforcement powers, 2:6-7
information under, 2:63-65
regulated areas, 2:6

Tenants' management
  organisations
    disputes, 2:87-88
    funding for, 2:78-79
    local authority support for, 2:83-84
    registration, 2:89
    right to manage, 2:81-82
    See also Management
Termination by tenant
  joint tenants,
    generally, 1:129-130
    surrender by, 1:126
  notice to quit,
    contents, 1:128
    effect, 1:129
    generally, 1:128
    joint tenants, 1:128
  surrender,
    agreement to surrender, 1:125
    examples, 1:126-128
    generally, 1:125
    joint tenants, by, 1:126
    operation of law, by, 1:126
Termination of tenancy agreement
  commencing possession proceedings, **4:8-13**
  length of notice, **4:13**
  notice seeking possession, **4:10-13**
Tied accommodation
  possession proceedings, **4:34-35**
  security of tenure and, 1:24, 1:88
Tort
  harassment, of, 3:33-35
  meaning, 3:101
  nuisance, of, 3:10
Transfer of tenancy
  security of tenure and, 1:8
Trespass to land
  private nuisance, as, 3:16
Trespasser
  county court procedure, 1:113
  licensee distinguished from, 1:113
  meaning, 1:11
  nature of, 1:113
  status of, 1:11
  unauthorised occupier, meaning, **4:158**
  See also Unauthorised occupier
Trial
  possession proceedings. *See* Possession proceedings
Two homes
  security of tenure, conditions for, 1:49-51

Unauthorised occupier
  meaning, **4:158**
  possession proceedings. *See* Possession proceedings
  See also Trespasser
Under-occupation
  possession proceedings, **4:42-43**
  secure tenant, grounds for possession against, 1:81-82
Undertaking
  annoyance, possession action based on, **4:110-112**
  meaning, **4:158**
  nuisance, possession action based on, **4:110-112**
  specimen form, **4:148-149**
Unless order
  meaning, **4:158**
  possession proceedings, **4:62-63**

Variation
  suspended possession order, terms of, 1:121
Victim
  harassment, of, assistance to, 3:88-89

Waiver of breach
  forfeiture and, 1:64

Waiver of breach – *cont*
secure tenant, grounds for possession against, 1:70
Warnings
nuisance, relating to, 3:39-40
Warrant
possession, for, 1:122, **4:134-135**
Waste
possession, ground for, 3:63-64
Wiring
faulty, as private nuisance, 3:17
Witness statements
meaning, **4:158**
possession proceedings,
annoyance, action based on, **4:110**
nuisance, action based on, **4:110**
pretrial procedure, **4:60-62**
Works
accommodation pending, 1:37, 1:77-78, **4:40-41**
landlord, of, 1:78-79, 1:84-85, **4:41**
Written agreement
tenancy, relating to, 1:8